AF255719

"By making these once-influential texts readily available, the series on early Christian apocrypha performs an invaluable service to scholars but also to any thoughtful reader interested in the breadth and diversity of the Christian tradition. The latest volume on the *Doctrine of Addai* is an excellent contribution, with a lucid translation grounded in thorough scholarly research. Long may this fine series continue."
> —Philip Jenkins, distinguished professor of history, Institute for Studies of Religion, Baylor University

"Through idiomatic translations of multiple Syriac, Greek, and Latin sources and a concise, yet comprehensive account of the development and transmission of the Abgar legend, Jacob Lollar has provided an invaluable tool for understanding how the Christians of Edessa fused civic history with sacred history to put Roman Mesopotamia at the very forefront of the apostolic tradition."
> —Kyle Smith, associate professor of historical studies and the study of religion, University of Toronto

"This excellent book is much more than a fresh translation of a foundational piece of Syriac literature—the earliest narrative on the arrival of Christianity to Edessa. The volume also comprises a sophisticated commentary, as well as the first systematic study of several inscriptions and papyri that attest the *Doctrine*, and of its textual afterlife over centuries. Jacob Lollar's work reshapes our understanding of the history of the *Doctrine*, its far-reaching impact on early Christians, and the role it played in later Syriac literature."
> —Alberto Rigolio, associate professor of classics, Durham University

"Probably composed in the early fifth century, the *Doctrina Addai* contains the earliest Syriac text of the famous written exchange between Jesus and the Edessene king Abgar V, along with a highly detailed account of the apostle Addai's subsequent mission to the kingdom. Let me applaud Jacob Lollar for his outstanding new English translation of this fascinating document."
> —William Adler, distinguished university professor of religious studies, North Carolina State University

"Jacob Lollar, one of the most competent experts in Syriac studies of his generation, not only offers us a careful translation and a very helpful introduction into the so-called Doctrine of Addai, but his volume also opens a door into the wider world of Syriac apocrypha. I am sure this book will make a fascinating text available to many fascinated readers."

—TOBIAS NICKLAS, chair for exegesis and hermeneutics of the New Testament, University of Regensburg

The Doctrine of Addai
and the Letters of Jesus and Abgar

TOOLS AND TRANSLATIONS

The Westar Tools and Translations series provides critical tools and fresh new translations for research on canonical and non-canonical texts that survive from the earliest periods of the Christian tradition to the Middle Ages. These writings are crucial for determining the complex history of Christian origins. The translations are known as the Scholars Version. Each work, whether a translation or research aid, is accompanied by textual notes, translation notes, cross references, and an index. An extensive introduction also sets out the challenge a text or research aid addresses.

EARLY CHRISTIAN APOCRYPHA

Editorial Board:
TONY BURKE
BRANDON HAWK
JANET SPITTLER

Translations of non-canonical texts out of the Christian tradition are offered as part of the Westar Tools and Translations series in cooperation with the North American Society for the Study of Christian Apocryphal Literature (NASS-CAL). The Early Christian Apocrypha series features fresh new translations of major apocryphal texts that survive from the early period of the Christian church. These non-canonical writings are crucial for determining the complex history of Christian origins. The series continues the work of Julian V. Hills, who edited the first six volumes of the series for Polebridge Press. *Studies in Christian Apocrypha* is a subseries to *Early Christian Apocrypha*. The subseries features studies (including short introductions, monographs, and thematic collections of essays) on Christian Apocrypha from any time period and in any of its myriad forms—from early "lost gospel" papyri, through medieval hagiography and sermons incorporating apocryphal traditions, up to modern apocryphal "forgeries."

Volume 1: *The Acts of Andrew*
Volume 2: *The Epistle of the Apostles*
Volume 3: *The Acts of Thomas*
Volume 4: *The Acts of Peter*
Volume 5: *Didache*
Volume 6: *The Acts of John*
Volume 7: *The Protevangelium of James*
Volume 8: *The Gospel of Pseudo-Matthew and the Nativity of the Virgin*
Volume 9: *The Apocryphal Gospels: Jesus Traditions Outside the Bible*
Volume 10: *The Doctrine of Addai and the Letters of Jesus and Abgar*

The Doctrine of Addai
and the Letters of Jesus and Abgar

Jacob A. Lollar

CASCADE *Books* · Eugene, Oregon

THE DOCTRINE OF ADDAI AND THE LETTERS OF JESUS AND ABGAR

Early Christian Apocrypha 10
Westar Tools and Translations

Cascade Books
An Imprint of Wipf and Stock Publishers
199 W. 8th Ave., Suite 3
Eugene, OR 97401

www.wipfandstock.com

PAPERBACK ISBN: 978-1-6667-5206-9
HARDCOVER ISBN: 978-1-6667-5207-6
EBOOK ISBN: 978-1-6667-5208-3

Cataloguing-in-Publication data:

Names: Lollar, Jacob A., author, translator.

Title: The Doctrine of Addai and the Letters of Jesus and Abgar / Jacob A. Lollar.

Description: Eugene, OR: Cascade Books, 2023. | Westar Tools and Translations. | Early Christian Apocrypha 10. | Includes bibliographical references and index.

Identifiers: ISBN 978-1-6667-5206-9 (paperback). | ISBN 978-1-6667-5207-6 (hardcover). | ISBN 978-1-6667-5208-3 (epub).

Subjects: LSCH: Abgar V, King of Edessa, 4 B.C–50 A.D. | Abgar Letters. | Apocryphal books (New Testament). | Manuscripts, Syriac. | Syriac language, texts.

Classification: BS2900 L66 2023 (print). | BS2900 (epub).

For Sarah

Contents

Acknowledgments | ix

List of Abbreviations | xi

Introduction | 1

1 The Doctrine of Addai | 31

2 Appendix A: The Development of the Abgar/Jesus Correspondence | 102

      Eusebius, *Ecclesiastical History* 1.121–22 | 102

      Egeria, *Itinerarium* 19.5–19 | 107

      Inscriptions | 109

      Papyri | 117

3 Appendix B: Further Developments of the Abgar/Jesus Tradition | 122

      Acts of Thaddaeus | 122

      Acts of Mār Māri | 124

      Epistles of Christ and Abgar | 126

Bibliography | 129

Index of Ancient Sources | 139

Index of Names and Places | 145

Acknowledgments

Reading the *Doctrine of Addai* was my first plunge into the abundant pool of Syriac literature and culture. It has occupied my thinking ever since and is one of the stories to which I continually find myself returning. At first, I suppose it was the startling realization, as a young seminary student, that there were traditions about Jesus writing something down in his own words—and it isn't even in the Bible! Now, I find myself captivated by the brilliance of the story as a peek into culture-building and mythmaking and how this resonates so well with what has taken place throughout the Christian tradition (and beyond) and is even now taking place in real time as people continually tell stories about themselves and their past. It is my persistent fascination with this story that ultimately compelled me to approach the editors about adding it to the *Early Christian Apocrypha* series. I am thankful for their support and trust in a young scholar to tackle this wondrously complex narrative.

I am indebted to so many people for their assistance in finishing this edition. First and foremost, I must thank Tony Burke, Brandon Hawk, and Janet Spittler who continue to support so many of us young scholars of Christian apocryphal literature and for working hard to keep the series going. Of all the sub-groups of scholarship to which I belong, the apocrypha people are my favorite. Without their generosity and encouragement—particularly during the pandemic—I doubt this volume would ever have happened. All the NASSCAL First Friday workshops, SBL Christian Apocrypha meetings, NASSCAL conferences, and other gatherings have been a plentiful spring of ideas, enrichment, and critical engagement. Thanks to everyone in these groups.

Specific people have offered helpful insights, critiques, and assistance along the way. Thanks to Brandon Hawk for proofreading my translation of Egeria's Latin—which was arguably the most difficult text to translate for this volume! Thanks to Blake Jurgens and Carson Bay for their valuable feedback on early drafts of the Introduction, and to J. Edward Walters for his helpful comments on the entire manuscript. My conversations over the years with Nathan Hardy, Gregory Given, and J. Edward Walters about the *Doctrine of Addai* have been very helpful in my thinking about the meaning, use, and history of this narrative. In 2017 I had the privilege of having lunch with Alain Desreumaux in Paris who kindly indulged my incessant questioning of everything from the date of the text to its continued legacy. More recently, I have benefitted from conversations with Tobias Nicklas about the importance of apocryphal texts for the shaping of Christian cultures. All of these people have been gracious with their time and insights, and I have profited from them all.

I must also thank my beginning Greek students at Abilene Christian University whose love of Greek led them to request translation projects for honors credits. To Reece Gardner, Dixie Jones, Spencer Kasselman, and Gabriel Laskey, thanks for all your work on the Greek texts of the Abgar/Jesus correspondence. Thanks also to my graduate assistant at the time, Matthew San Miguel, who worked tirelessly in typing out and comparing all the Greek texts for me. And a shout out to the workers at Grain Theory in Abilene, Texas for putting up with books scattered over tables. Thanks for keeping the coffee and beer flowing!

As always, my greatest debt is to my family. To my daughters, Kora and Maryn: thank you for putting up with many evenings of me saying, "Hang on, let me finish this." Well, I'm finished! To my wife, Sarah: thanks for supporting me through the roughest few years of our life together, with the pandemic, terrible job markets, and moves across town and across the world. This book—and every other one I write—is for you.

Jacob A. Lollar
Regensburg, Germany
Spring 2022

Abbreviations

Ancient

Acts Māri	*Acts of Mār Māri*
Acts Pet.	*Acts of Peter*
Acts Phil.	*Acts of Philip*
Acts Thad.	*Acts of Thaddaeus*
1 Apoc. Jas.	*1 Revelation of James*
Ascen. Isa.	*Ascension of Isaiah*
Augustine	
Cons.	*De consensus evangelistarum*
Epist.	*Epistulae*
Faust.	*Contra Faustum Manichaeum*
Haer.	*De haeresibus*
Bardaisan	
Bk. Laws	*Book of the Laws of Countries*
Cassius Dio	
Hist.	*Roman History*
Chron. Ed.	*Chronicle of Edessa*
Chron Zuq.	*Chronicle of Zuqnīn*
Cod. Theod.	*Theodosian Codes*
Cyril of Alexandria	
Ep.	*Epistulae*
Doctr. Addai	*Doctrine of Addai*
Egeria	
Itin.	*Itinerarium*
1 En.	*1 Enoch*

Ephrem
    Azym.   *de Azymis (On the Unleavened Bread)*
    Cruc.   *de Crucifixion (On the Crucifixion)*
    Eccl.   *de Ecclesia (On the Church)*
    Haer.   *Contra Haereses*
    Hyp. 5   *Fifth Discourse to Hypatius*
    Jul.   *Contra Julianum*
    Nis.   *Carmina Nisibena*
Ep. Chr. Abg.   *Epistles of Christ and Abgar*
Eusebius
    Hist. eccl.   *Ecclesiastical History*
Evagrius Scholasticus
    Hist. eccl.   *Ecclesiastical History*
Gos. Pet.   *Gospel of Peter*
Hist. John   *(Syriac) History of John*
Hist. Paul   *History of Paul*
Hist. Phil.   *History of Philip*
Hist. Sim. Ceph.   *History of Simon Cephas, Chief of the Apostles*
Josephus
    A.J.   *Jewish Antiquities*
    J.W.   *Jewish War*
Jub.   *Jubilees*
Mart. Ait.   *Martyrdom of Aitalaha*
Mart. Bars.   *Martyrdom of Barsamya*
Mart. Nars.   *Martyrdom of Narsai the Ascetic*
Mart. Sharb.   *Martyrdom of Sharbel*
Porphyry
    Vit. Plot.   *Vita Plotini*
Pre. Pet. Rome   *Preaching of Simon Cephas in the City of Rome*
Procopius
    Wars   *History of the Wars*
Rabbula
    Admon.   *Admonitions for the Monks*
    Comm. Admon.   *Commandments and Admonitions for the Priests and Children of the Covenant*
Solomon of Basra
    Bk. Bee   *Book of the Bee*

Suetonius	
Claud.	*Divus Claudius*
Tacitus	
Ann.	*Annals*
Teach. Apos.	*Teaching of the Apostles*
Theodoret	
Hist. eccl.	*Ecclesiastical History*
Vit. Eph.	*Vita Ephrem*
Vit. Rab.	*Vita Rabbula*
Wis	Wisdom of Solomon

Modern

AcOr	*Acta Orientalia*
AnBoll	*Analecta Bollandiana*
ARG	*Archiv für Religionsgeschichte*
Aug	*Augustinianum*
BCH	*Bulletin de correspondence hellénique*
BHT	Beiträge zur historischen Theologie
CCSA	Corpus Christianorum: Series Apocryphorum
CSCO	Corpus Scriptorum Christianorum Orientalium
CTJ	*Calvin Theological Journal*
CWS	Classics of Western Spirituality
GEDSH	*Gorgias Encyclopedic Dictionary of the Syriac Heritage.* Edited by Sebastian Brock, et al. Piscataway, NJ: Gorgias Press 2011.
HTR	*Harvard Theological Review*
JCoptS	*Journal of Coptic Studies*
JHS	*Journal of Hellenic Studies*
JJS	*Journal of Jewish Studies*
JNES	*Journal of Near Eastern Studies*
JTS	*Journal of Theological Studies*
LCL	Loeb Classical Library
MNTA	*New Testament Apocrypha: More Noncanonical Scriptures.* Vol. 1 edited by Tony Burke and Brent Landau. Vols. 2 and 3 edited by Tony Burke. Grand Rapids: Eerdmans, 2016, 2019, 2022
Mus	*Le Muséon*

NovT	*Novum Testamentum*
NPNF2	*Nicene and Post-Nicene Fathers, Series 2*. 14 vols. Edited by Henry Wace and Philip Schaff. New York: Christian Literature Company, 1885–1899.
NTS	*New Testament Studies*
OCP	*Orientalia Christiana Periodica*
OECS	Oxford Early Christian Studies
OLA	Orientalia Lovanensia Periodica
ParOr	*Parole de l'Orient*
REG	*Revue des études grecques*
SBLTT	SBL Texts and Translations
SC	Sources chrétiennes
SecCent	*Second Century*
StPB	Studia Post-biblica
VC	*Vigiliae Christianae*
WGRW	Writings from the Greco-Roman World
ZS	*Zeitschrift für Semitistik und verwandte Gebiete*
ZWT	*Zeitschrift für wissenschaftliche Theologie*

Manuscripts and Sigla

A	St. Petersburg, National Library of Russia, Siriys-kaya novaya seria 4 (5th/6th cent.)
B	London, British Library, Add. 14644 (5th cent.)
C	London, British Library, Add. 14654 (5th cent.)
D	London, British Library, Add. 14535 (9th cent.)

Introduction

In chapter 2 of the New Testament book of Acts, the followers of Jesus gather at Pentecost and begin speaking in tongues. The crowd around them is amazed to hear them speaking in their own languages. A list is given of all the different nationalities and languages present: Parthians, Medes, Elamites, and residents of Mesopotamia, Judea, Cappadocia, Pontus and Asia, Phrygia, Pamphylia, Egypt, Libya, Rome, Crete, and Arabia (2:9–11). At first glance, it is obvious that one of these things is not like the other: Rome is the only European city represented in this list. Indeed, if we were to take Acts 2 as our only source for this period of Christian history, we might think that the future of the movement lay in the East, expanding out from Jerusalem into North Africa and continental Asia. Despite this first impression, however, the mission of Paul quickly takes over in the Acts narrative, and Paul heads west, stopping off in Greece and Macedonia and eventually heading to Rome.[1]

What about those Eastern peoples at Pentecost? What about the expansion of Christianity in the East? Acts gives some information about Syria, Asia Minor, and even about Galatia and Pontus, but tells us nothing about North Africa, Arabia, Mesopotamia, or Parthia—let alone about Media, India, or further still, China. Nevertheless, Christianity did make its way into these regions and flourished.[2] For more than a millennium Christians in the Middle East and Asia thrived and developed distinct

---

1. Later traditions and apostolic narratives have Paul reaching Spain before being executed in Rome. See, e.g., Lollar, "History of Paul."

2. An approachable study of Christianity in Asia and North Africa can be found in Jenkins, *Lost History of Christianity*. More detailed scholarly treatments of this expansion may be found in Briquel-Chatonnet and Debié, *Le monde syriaque*; and King, *Syriac World*.

forms of Christian doctrine, piety, and literature.[3] They prospered, at times, alongside their Sassanian and Arab neighbors, well before the Western renaissance ushered in by the coronation of Charlemagne in 800.

Prior to the fourth century, we have precious little evidence of demographics of Christians in the eastern regions and Mesopotamia.[4] No New Testament figure ever writes to or visits any of the Mesopotamian cities[5] and the reference to the Middle Eastern and Mesopotamian locales in Acts 2 amount to almost nothing in the course of the narrative. The Christians in the East, in short, saw nothing of themselves and their heritage in this text. But this did not deter them. They began to make their own stories, placing themselves and their local histories within sacred history. By late antiquity, Christians in Asia and Mesopotamia began linking their communities and their heritage to various figures. Some wrote stories about the Magi who visit the infant Jesus (Matt 2);[6] others traced their lineage back to other apostles who play little or no role in the Acts narrative, such as Judas Thomas,[7] Thaddaeus,[8] and Philip.[9] One of the most famous of the apostles who worked in these eastern regions was known in Syriac as Addai.

---

3. See, e.g., Tannous, *Making of the Medieval Middle East.*

4. On this problem see the recent essay by Taylor, "Coming of Christianity."

5. One exception is 1 Peter, which is written to exiles in "Babylon"; however, this is likely a reference to Rome, the destroyer of the temple in the author's time.

6. See Jullien and Jullien, *Apôtres des confins*, 111–17; Landau, *Revelation of the Magi*, 28–34; and Vanden Eykel, *Magi*, 66–88.

7. See Klijn, *Acts of Thomas*; and Andrade, *Journey of Christianity*. Judas Thomas is linked to the evangelization of Edessa as well as to India. Some modern South Indian Christian groups, such as the Malabar Catholic Church, the Chaldean Syrian Church, the Malankara Syriac Orthodox Church, the Malankara Catholic Church, the Malabar Independent Syrian Church, and the Mar Thoma Syrian Church still maintain their traditional links to Judas Thomas as the founder of Christianity in India.

8. See Palmer, "*Logos* of the Mandylion." In Eusebius's account (*Hist. eccl.* 1.13), the apostle Thomas sent Thaddaeus, named as one of the 72 sent out as missionaries by Jesus in Luke 10:1–20, as the evangelist to Edessa. This link is further established by the sixth-century *Acts of Thaddaeus*, which claims that Thaddaeus originally came from Edessa and then returned to evangelize.

9. See Bovon and Matthews, *Acts of Philip*. According to *Acts Phil.*, the apostle eventually settles and dies in the Syrian city of Mabbug (Hieropolis), which had ecclesiastical ties to Edessa. There is a unique Syriac legend of Philip (the *History of Philip*) that is distinct from *Acts Phil.* In *Hist. Phil.* the apostle sails to Carthage (or Carthagene) and performs a number of feats to rid the city of Jews and pagans. A new study of this text is forthcoming in the CSCO series. See Ruani and Villey, "Recherches"; and Ruani, "Peut-on parler de *testimonia.*" See Kitchen, "History of Philip," for a recent English translation.

The *Doctrine of Addai* claims to be an official account of Christianity's arrival in Mesopotamia through the ministry of Addai (sometimes called Thaddaeus), one of Jesus' apostles (see Mark 6:18//Matt 10:3). The beginning of *Doctr. Addai* preserves the epistolary correspondence of Jesus with King Abgar of Edessa (known in Syriac as Urhay, modern Şanlıurfa, Turkey), an exchange that has captured the imaginations of Christians for centuries. Due in part to its longstanding popularity, the correspondence of Abgar and Jesus has played a prominent, albeit contested role in historical reconstructions of Christian expansion into Mesopotamia and the East. Whereas some scholars have dismissed nearly the entire narrative as a complete fabrication of a later period, others have attempted to tease out fragments of historicity from the story. Such disparities of opinion are hardly a product of modern skepticism. Church historians from late antiquity and the Middle Ages were just as divided as their contemporary counterparts regarding the authenticity of both the Abgar/Jesus correspondence and the narrative that follows in *Doctr. Addai* and other related texts. Many late antique and medieval believers were undeterred by the opinions of historians with regard to the significance and popularity of the letters and the story—and their popularity continued well into the modern period.[10]

While Edessa was an important city in many respects in the ancient world, nowhere does the New Testament explicitly associate it with the earliest stages of the Christian movement. The silence of the New Testament, however, did little to diminish the popularity of the story of Abgar and Jesus and the conversion of a chief city in the East. Christians on the eastern frontier of the Roman Empire created the correspondence to construct their past and forge new identities by writing themselves into the annals of Christian history. The final stage of that process was a narrative written in Syriac, the native language of the area around Edessa, called the *Doctrine of Addai.*

---

10. Eusebius (*Hist. eccl.* 1.13) seems to regard the letters as authentic and says he took them and the narrative epilogue from the archives of Edessa. Procopius (*Wars* 2.12.25–26) has some reservations about their authenticity, as does Evagrius Scholasticus (*Hist. eccl.* 4.27). Augustine (*Epist.* 230; *Faust.* 28.4; *Cons.* 1.7.11) regarded the letters as inauthentic and apocryphal. See Given, "Utility and Variance." One British historian wrote in 1798 that "the common people in England have [the correspondence of Abgar and Jesus] in their houses, in many places, fixed in a frame with our Savior's picture before it; and they generally with much honesty and devotion regard it as the word of God, and the genuine Epistle of Christ" (Jones, *New and Full Method,* 2:2).

Summary

Doctr. Addai takes as its starting point the Abgar/Jesus correspondence. The opening line of the story, as it has been preserved in the only complete manuscript of the composition, directly connects the narrative to the letters it claims to preserve: "The letter of King Abgar, son of King Ma'nu, when he sent it to our Lord in Jerusalem, and when Addai the apostle came to him in Urhay." The story is set in the 343rd year of the Greeks which, following the Seleucid calendar (as many Syriac scribes did for generations), corresponds to the year 31/32 CE. It thus purports to take place during the reign of Abgar Ukkāmā ("the Black") of Edessa and during the last few years of Jesus' life and ministry.

Following this introduction, we learn that Abgar, having heard about Jesus, sends several messengers to Palestine to learn more about him. After these messengers—Māryāhb, Šmešgrām, and Ḥanan the archivist—report back to Abgar, the king then sends Ḥanan back to Jesus with a letter, begging him to come to Edessa and heal him from a long-term illness (gout, according to later traditions). Abgar also offers Jesus refuge in Edessa from the Jews who were seeking to kill him. Ḥanan delivers the letter to Jesus, who gives him a reply to pass on to Abgar (it is unclear if this reply was written down or just spoken). In his response, Jesus declines Abgar's request, saying that he must remain in Judea to complete his mission for which he was sent by God. He promises, however, to send one of his disciples to Edessa to fulfill Abgar's requests. After Jesus' ascension, Judas Thomas sends one of the seventy-two disciples, a man named Addai, to Edessa, in order to bring Jesus' promise to fruition.

Upon Addai's arrival in Edessa, he stays at the home of a Jewish man named Tobia. When his presence is revealed to Abgar, Addai is brought before the king and heals Abgar as well as some others among the nobility, thereby proving he is Jesus' messenger. Abgar rejoices and brings his family and the Edessene nobility to witness Addai's powers. Addai is then invited to proclaim the gospel to the court. He begins with an anecdotal story about the finding of the True Cross by Protonike, the wife of Emperor Claudius, an example of another ruler who came to faith in Jesus. Abgar and the court are amazed at the story and marshal the entire city to come and hear Addai's preaching.

Addai then lays out his teaching, which makes up the bulk of the narrative (chs. 36–61). He gives an account of Jesus' deeds and, in particular, encourages all to come to faith by abandoning their ancestral worship. His message is well received and most of the city converts, including a number of the priests of local cults, who tear down the altars to their gods. Addai builds a church and then appoints several of the local leaders as priests. People from all over Mesopotamia begin to hear about Addai and his teaching, including merchants on the Silk Road and even King Narseh of the Persians. Abgar writes a letter to Emperor Tiberius encouraging him to investigate the situation of the Jews in Palestine who murdered Jesus. Tiberius writes back that he has already punished the Jews and acknowledges Jesus' significance.

Addai then establishes the episcopate in Edessa, building more churches and appointing people to various offices. Soon after, however, he falls ill and offers his final testament to the nobility (chs. 78–91). He then lays his hands on Aggai, one of Addai's first converts, ordaining him as his successor. After bidding farewell to Abgar, Addai dies. Abgar and the entire city mourn Addai and set up a memorial festival in his honor. The new church flourishes under Aggai, until one of the sons of Abgar comes to power and has Aggai killed. Since Aggai had not been able to ordain a successor, Palūt—another one of Addai's disciples—must travel to Antioch to be ordained by Bishop Serapion. The story ends with a note that the preceding account of the teaching of Addai had been written down by the scribe Lebubnā and placed in the city's archives.

Provenance, Date, Authorship

It is with Eusebius of Caesarea that the literary accounts of the Abgar/Jesus correspondence and, later, *Doctr. Addai* find their origins. When Eusebius composed his *Ecclesiastical History* in 325 CE he claimed to have seen an exchange written in the "language of the Syrians" (ἐκ τῆς Σύρων φωνῆς)[11] between Jesus and King Abgar the Black of Edessa (r. 4 BCE–7 CE and 13–50 CE) (*Hist. eccl.* 1.13). Eusebius presents the entire correspondence in Greek and then provides a short narrative that he says was appended to the letters, also in the "language of the Syrians" (τῇ Σύρων φωνῇ). In this narrative, Judas Thomas appoints Thaddaeus, said to be one of the seventy(-two) from Luke 10, to go to Edessa and heal Abgar and preach the gospel there.

Doctr. Addai is probably an original Syriac narrative, even though the earliest traces of it come from the Greek text of Eusebius. The text undoubtedly originated in Edessa: the story is set in this city and the manuscripts

11. On the development of Syriac as a literary language, see Rigolio, "Syriac," 167–78.

that contain the text were most likely copied there. The fictive author, Lebubnā, claims it was placed in the civic archives (see ch. 103), the same place that Eusebius says he read the letters and translated them. Some modern historians have questioned Eusebius's claim. Recent linguistic comparisons, however, have supported the likelihood that Eusebius was telling the truth, even if he himself was not the one who actually performed the translation.[12] Further substantiating the claim that the letters were part of the civic archives of Edessa is the late fourth century travelogue of the Christian pilgrim Egeria. In her account of her visit to Edessa in 384 CE, Egeria says that the letters of Abgar and Jesus were in the city and the local bishop even read them aloud to her (*Itin.* 16). Egeria then reveals:

> It also gave me great joy that I received from the holy man the letters of Abgar to the Lord and of the Lord to Abgar, which the holy bishop had read to us. While I have copies at home, it gave me great joy that I received them here from him also, since perhaps a lesser version has come to our home, because what I received here is in fact longer. If our Lord Jesus allows and I return home, you shall read it, my dear ladies. (*Itin.* 19, my trans.)[13]

Egeria's statement confirms that the letters of Abgar and Jesus had been copied and transmitted as far as Spain, likely due to their inclusion in Eusebius's *History*. Her comment also reveals that there were multiple versions of the letters in circulation—a fact that is borne out in the epigraphic evidence included in this volume. Additionally, Egeria's testimony substantiates Eusebius's claim that there were copies of the letters at Edessa. Since both Eusebius and Egeria testify that the letters were in Edessa, there is little reason to doubt that they were in the city. Moreover, there is no reason to doubt that the letters originated in Edessa (though perhaps not in the city's archive), since they are directly involved with the city's political and religious institutions. The "nationalistic" tone of the *Doctr. Addai*, with its clear interest in Edessa's ecclesiastical structure, strongly suggests that it likewise originated in Edessa.

12. See Polański, "Translation, Amplification, Paraphrase," 164–72, 175–86. Polański uses the versions from *Doctr. Addai* for his comparison. I am not convinced that the letters as they appear in *Doctr. Addai* are the earliest possible form of the letters in Syriac, but they are the earliest extant Syriac versions. Brock ("Eusebius and Syriac Christianity," 213) thinks it unlikely that Eusebius made the translation. Brock also doubts that these documents would have been kept in the city's archives, as Eusebius claims.

13. Excerpts from Egeria are taken from Appendix A in this volume; consult the appendix for information about the editions used for the translation.

The date of the composition of *Doctr. Addai* requires further investigation. Most scholars are convinced that the final form of *Doctr. Addai* appeared in the first part of the fifth century. Its component parts, however, come from as early as the third century. Although it is a debatable issue, the origins of a story about a "King Abgar of Edessa" converting to "Christianity" may reflect the reign of Abgar VIII the Great, who ruled from 177 to 212 CE. This connection with Abgar VIII, the last prominent Abgarid ruler, might be further established by the role of Palūt in the story, who, as the successor of Addai and Aggai, receives ordination from Bishop Serapion of Antioch, who in turn had received his own ordination from Zephyrinus of Rome (ch. 102). This marks one of many serious chronological errors appearing throughout the text, since Serapion's tenure at Antioch began in 189 or 192 CE, whereas Zephyrinus's tenure at Rome began in 202 CE.[14] While the chronologies fail to establish a convincing link to the first century when Addai purportedly lived, they do coincide with the reign of Abgar the Great quite nicely. Several scholars have hypothesized oral traditions which (intentionally?) conflate Abgar VIII (the real first Abgarid convert to Christianity) with Abgar Ukkāmā who reigned during the lifetime of Jesus.[15]

The figure of Palūt appears to have been a historical leader of one Christian sect in Edessa probably in the early part of the fourth century.[16] Ephrem mentions him as a principal figure of the Christians in Edessa whom Ephrem considered to be the "orthodox" Christians.[17] By introducing Palūt into the mythical story of Addai and Abgar, the "Palūtian" Christians (as Ephrem identifies them) sought to forge a link between the apostolic past and their more recent cultural memory. Steven Ross summarizes the situation nicely:

> The best explanation is probably to assume that considerations of chronology simply buckled under the strong desire of the 'Palutian' Christians (who did have a connection with the Antiochene church) to enhance their status within the community by the claim to apostolic authority.[18]

---

14. See Brock, "Eusebius," 227–28.

15. See Palmer, "King Abgar"; and Burkitt, *Early Eastern Christianity*.

16. Fiano, "Trinitarian Controversies."

17. Ephrem mentions Christians going by the name "Palutians" in *Haer.* 22.5–6. See Griffith, "Marks of the 'True Church,'" 129–30.

18. Ross, *Roman Edessa*, 134.

We may suggest, therefore, that the parts of the narrative that feature Palūt originate from the fourth-century traditions and groups who venerated him as a leading figure of the "Palūtian" sect of Christianity in Edessa.

Another important name in the early traditions of *Doctr. Addai* is Thomas. Egeria makes no mention of Addai nor the events recorded in *Doctr. Addai*; however, she does discuss veneration of Judas Thomas in Edessa and her visit to his shrine in the city. Andrew Palmer suggests that, given the role played by Thomas in both the Eusebian story and *Doctr. Addai*, there may have been a version of the story of Edessa's evangelization in which Thomas played the role of the apostle sent to the city (see also Figure 1 below).[19] Such a hypothesis is plausible, but the silence of Egeria regarding Addai and *Doctr. Addai* is not a sure indication of the absence of the Addai traditions in Edessa at that time.

Possibly more revealing about the date of at least part of the narrative is the appearance of an additional line in Jesus' response to Abgar that is not mentioned by Eusebius. In *Doctr. Addai*, Jesus ends his reply to Abgar saying, "Now, for your city: may it be blessed and may no enemy ever again have authority over it" (5:6). This remark by Jesus came to be understood by late antique Christians as a promise of divine protection claimed by cities all over the empire against any kind of attack, be it enemies, sickness, or even the presence of demons.[20] The sixth-century historian Procopius recognized that this promise of Jesus was an addition not found in Eusebius's version:

> When the Christ says this message, he wrote in reply to Augarus (i.e., Abgar), saying distinctly that he would not come, but promising him health in the letter. And they say that he added this also that never would the city be liable to capture by the barbarians. This final portion of the letter was entirely unknown to those who wrote the history of that time; for they did not even make mention of it anywhere; but the men of Edessa say that they found it with the letter, so that they have even caused the letter to be inscribed in this form on the gates of the city instead of any other defense. (*Wars* 2.12.25–26; trans. Dewing, LCL)[21]

19. Palmer, "King Abgar," 29. The inscription from the "Forty Caverns/Tombs" in Edessa (see item 3.2 in Appendix A) conflates the figures of Thaddaeus and Thomas, which gives credibility to Palmer's theory about a Thomas version of the legend.

20. See Given, "Utility and Variance."

21. It is worth noting that Procopius knows this additional line only from inscriptions he saw, not from a literary text.

Procopius is correct that the earliest version from Eusebius lacks Jesus' promise. However, several of the inscriptions translated in the Appendices contain the promise of protection and appear to date to the fourth century, meaning that this addition was already spreading during this time. In fact, it was known by the time of Egeria, who writes:

> Then the holy bishop told me the following story about this water: "After King Abgar wrote a letter to the Lord and the Lord wrote back through Ananias the courier, just as it is written in the letter, the Persians, at a much later time, came down upon us and surrounded the city. Immediately Abgar took the Lord's letter with his whole army to the gate and prayed aloud and said, "Lord Jesus, you promised us that no enemies would enter this city; see, now, how the Persians attack us!" After saying this, the king held up the letter openly in his upraised hand, and suddenly, outside the city, so great a darkness fell over the eyes of the Persians, who had already come three miles outside the city, and the darkness was so confusing to them that they could scarcely set up camp and patrol even three miles outside of the city. (*Itin.* 8–9; my trans.)

Given the presence of Jesus' promise of protection in the letter read to Egeria, it must have been added sometime between Eusebius's completion of the *Ecclesiastical History* (around 325) and 384.[22]

The insertion of this line into Jesus's letter probably occurred in Edessa. A likely catalyst for its addition was the failed campaign into Persia by the emperor Julian in 363.[23] The Roman army was cut down and Julian was fatally wounded, forcing the army to retreat to the fortress city of Nisibis. Upon his ascension, the new emperor Jovian ceded Nisibis and a number of other territories to the Persians. At this point, Nisibis was a bastion of Christianity, producing leaders like the bishop Jacob who attended the Council of Nicaea in 325 and, of course, Ephrem, one of Jacob's deacons. After the city was ceded to the Persians, Shapur II allowed the Christian population to leave peacefully with the Roman army. Many of these Nisibene refugees, including Ephrem, ended up in Edessa.

Among the many famous stories about Nisibis was one involving Bishop Jacob and the Persian army. Shapur II besieged Nisibis in 337/338,

---

22. It is possible, of course, that this line was present in some versions of the letters prior to 325, in which case Eusebius either had a version in which the promise was omitted, or he omitted the promise himself.

23. See Mirkovic, *Prelude to Constantine*, 35–36.

but his efforts resulted in failure. The story is recounted by the fifth-century historian Theodoret:

> The next day [Shapur II] attacked [Nisibis] in full force, and looked to enter the city through the breaches that had been made. But he found the wall built up on both sides, and all his labour vain. For that holy man (i.e., Jacob), through prayer, filled with valour both the troops and the rest of the townsfolk, and both built the walls, withstood the engines, and beat off the advancing foe. And all this he did without approaching the walls, but by beseeching the Lord of all within the church . . . the excellent Ephraim (he is the best writer among the Syrians) besought the divine Jacobus to mount the wall to see the barbarians and to let fly at them the darts of his curse. So the divine man consented and climbed up into a tower but when he saw the innumerable host he discharged no other curse than that mosquitoes and gnats might be sent forth upon them, so that by means of these tiny animals they might learn the might of the Protector of the Romans. On his prayer followed clouds of mosquitoes and gnats; they filled the hollow trunks of the elephants, and the ears and nostrils of horses and other animals. (*Hist. eccl.* 2.30; trans. Jackson, modified)

This story sounds remarkably similar to the one told to Egeria about Edessa. In both cases, the Persians surrounded the city, a Christian leader appealed to God, and God routed the enemy in a miraculous way. Nisibis had procured a reputation for divine favor, a prestige that was even a source of pride for Ephrem.[24] God would not allow Nisibis to be taken, until, Ephrem argues, their judgment lapsed by allowing "pagan" cultic sites to be reopened at Julian's command (*Jul.* 1.8–15). Their city was gone, and with it the pride of the Nisibene Christians. Their new city, however, offered a hopeful opportunity. The Nisibene refugees provided the idea of God's protection over Edessa for the myth of Abgar. They synthesized the prestige of Nisibis's perpetual divine protection and the foundation myth

---

24. Cf. *Nis.* 1.11 where Ephrem compares Nisibis to Noah's ark sheltering the inhabitants from the deluge, and to Christ's resurrection on the third day—this being the third siege against the city in Ephrem's lifetime: [Nisibis speaking] "Grant not victory over Your beloved to the Evil One || whose avarice you [defeated] twice and three times. || Allow my victory to fly over the whole world || to acquire glory for You in the whole world. || O He Who was revived the third [day], || put me not to death in the third [trial]!" (trans. from McVey, *Ephrem*, 16–17).

of Christian Edessa, so that, in Drijvers' words, "Edessa is presented as the true heir of Nisibis's glorious Christian past."[25]

If the letters of Abgar and Jesus had been in Edessa since before Eusebius wrote his history, it was not until after the arrival of Nisibene refugees in 363 CE that the letters began to take on new meanings for the Christians there. It is likely at this time that the myth of Christian origins in Edessa that would become *Doctr. Addai* began to take shape. The story is a quasi-nationalist retelling of Edessa's Christian history that legitimizes a particular brand of Christianity within the city while both overtly and symbolically delegitimizing other religious groups, including other Christianities.[26] The specific mention of the fall of the cults of Bel and Nebo (ch. 67), the cult of Sin (ch. 50), and Atargatis (ch. 50), all of whom were prominent deities in Edessa into the fifth century, are overt examples of *Doctr. Addai's* interest in promoting Christianity over other cults at the time of the text's composition.

There are thus elements of *Doctr. Addai* that reach back probably into the third century and others that develop in the fourth century. The text as we know it must have developed at the end of the fourth century at the earliest, but more likely reached its final form in the first half of the fifth century, as the contextual elements I analyze below suggest. Despite what Eusebius and the author of *Doctr. Addai* would have readers believe, the

25. Drijvers ("Syriac Romance of Julian," 211) argues that the *Julian Romance* was produced by the Nisibene refugees in the late fourth century. This date can no longer be defended (see Mazzola and Van Nuffelen, "*Julian Romance*," for the date). Drijvers is certainly right in his observations concerning the projection of Nisibis's past onto Edessa's. See also the comment by Segal (*Edessa*, 75): "The thought of Nisibis was probably present in their minds, if we may judge from the bishop's account to Egeria of the miraculous deliverance of Edessa from the Persians. His story is wholly inappropriate to Edessa." The imported reputation of Edessa became a lasting symbol. The *Julian Romance* (123–24) maintains the idea that Edessa will never be conquered in its reflection on this period of Edessa's history: "Christ is the king of Edessa, and He dwells in its citadels. No foreigner is exalted above Him. If Edessa did not open its gates to the strong kings of Assyria, when they besieged it for three years and did not subdue it, will Edessa open its gates and greet you, the Mad One, the contemptable foreigner, the worshiper of idols? Heaven forbid, that your unclean feet which trod the thresholds of pagan temples should step in the streets of the 'Blessed One'. Draw your sword against us and stretch your bow as much as you wish. We will not be weary in your war. We have someone who stands at our head and who fights in our stead" (trans. Sokoloff).

26. On the inter-religious and intra-religious conflicts in Edessa during the fourth century, see Shepardson, *Anti-Judaism*.

authenticity of the Abgar/Jesus correspondence in the first century cannot be maintained.

Alexander Mirkovic argues for two basic phases of composition: pre-Great Persecution (303 CE) and post-Great Persecution (313 CE). The first phase was essentially an oral phase, though it may have included a (now lost) written form of the legend which Mirkovic calls the Early Syriac Version (ESV). In this phase are included traditions associating Judas Thomas with the conversion of Edessa (known by Egeria);[27] traditions about the conversion of a "King Abgar" (known from Bardaisan's *Books of the Laws of the Countries*); and traditions about Addai, who was a disciple sent before a king to preach a new doctrine (known from stories of Mani's disciple Addai; discussed below).[28] All of these traditions influenced the formation of the ESV. Mirkovic's second phase is essentially the fourth century, in which we find abundant written testimony to the story by Eusebius and Egeria. Eusebius borrows from both the Thomas traditions and from the ESV in constructing his version of the story, whereas Egeria also shows influences of the Thomas tradition and her account contains the added line about Edessa's divine protection. Mirkovic argues that several other parts of the story were added in the course of the fourth century, including the Abgar/Tiberius correspondence (chs. 74–75), the Abgar/Narses correspondence (ch. 73), the Protonike legend (chs. 16–30), Addai's sermons (chs. 36–61; 78–97), and the mention of Aggai and Palūt as Addai's successors (chs. 97, 102). Mirkovic leaves out of his analysis the epigraphic references to the Abgar/Jesus correspondence from the fourth century, some of which include the formula of protection. The editorial process culminated in the final version of *Doctr. Addai* probably before the death of Rabbula in 435 CE (see Figure 1).

27. Palmer ("King Abgar," 29) argues that Thomas was the apostle in the "original" version of the legend.

28. Mirkovic, *Prelude to Constantine*, 21–22.

FIGURE 1: THE TRANSMISSION OF THE ADDAI LEGEND

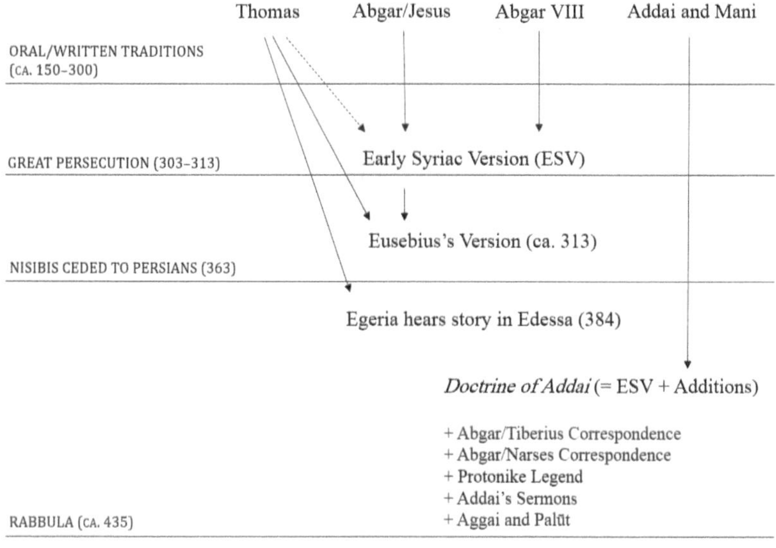

The blending of the various elements into what is now *Doctr. Addai* was done with precision and imagination. As to who could have done so, we are left with only a few clues. The writer claims to be Lebubnā, the king's scribe and associate of Ḥanan the archivist. This may be the real name of a fourth- or fifth-century scribe, but the person has clearly inserted himself into an imagined Edessene past. As Mirkovic observes:

> In looking at the text, one gets the impression that 'Labubna' is not quite certain how to represent the Roman world in the distant past. He simply assumes that the world created by Diocletian and Constantine always existed and shuffles only a few pieces of information he possesses about classical antiquity.[29]

With the person of "Lebubnā" it is probably best to think of an editor who was, perhaps, responsible for blending the various elements of the story from fragments of tradition and text. In all likelihood, this person was a monk writing in the region of Edessa. He clearly understood the christological debates raging in his time and takes a firm position on some of them. He also appears to have been profoundly bothered by the existence of any religious group but his own in Edessa. It is the Nicene Christianity of his ilk that he intends to convince his readers was the "original" Christianity in

---

29. Mirkovic, *Prelude to Constantine*, 78.

Edessa. A glimpse into the detailed context of the late fourth and early fifth centuries may provide further insights into why "Lebubnā" tried so hard to convince his readers of his myth of origins for Christianity in Oshroene.

Historical Context

There are traces of inner-Christian debates in the narrative that provide hints about situations happening in Edessa in the latter half of the fourth century. *Doctr. Addai* has a very clear pro-Nicene theology (see chs. 36–45 especially) and may represent, in the words of Emanuel Fiano, "the ripe fruit, and the later literary crystallization, of regional processes of ecclesiastical centralization and increasing connection between church hierarchies and imperial power, which had found a crucial catalyst in the fourth-century Trinitarian controversies."[30] The mention of Palūt as a successor of Addai suggests a conscious alignment with the "Palūtian" (see ch. 102) faction of Christianity in the city, one with which Ephrem specifically aligned himself.[31]

Doctr. Addai targets other Christian sects in the city, in particular Manichaeans, who had deep roots in Edessa. Han J.W. Drijvers argues convincingly for the targeting of Manichaeans in the *Doctr. Addai*[32] and Alain Desreumaux has traced many of the critiques of Manichaeism in the text,[33] but one of the more important ones is the name of the main protagonist, Addai. Neither Eusebius nor Egeria mention the name Addai. Drijvers argues that the name is actually a play on the name of a famous disciple of Mani, Adda/Addai, who also presented himself before a king and converted him to the "true faith."[34] However, Nils Pedersen argues, *contra* Drijvers, that the name Addai, which appears also in *1 Revelation of James*, had already been a part of the Syriac traditions as early as the ESV.[35] Pedersen thus suggests

---

30. Fiano, "Trinitarian Controversies," 109. On the fourth-century ecclesiastical debates in Edessa see also Shepardson, *Anti-Judaism*.

31. Griffith, "Marks of the 'True Church.'"

32. See Drijvers, "Jews and Christians at Edessa"; and Drijvers, "Facts and Problems."

33. Desreumaux, "La figure du roi Abgar d'Édesse," 36–40.

34. Drijvers, "Addai und Mani."

35. See Pedersen, "Legendary Addai." Although he does not mention Mirkovic's work, Pedersen comes to a similar conclusion about an early Syriac version that predates Eusebius, which Pedersen labels "pre-*DA*."

that the name Addai is much older and that both *Doctr. Addai* and *1 Apoc. Jas.* are drawing on similar traditions.

While the appearance of the name Addai in *1 Apoc. Jas.* is interesting and raises a number of questions (e.g., is this the same Addai imagined in *Doctr. Addai*, as Pedersen claims?), it does not, on the whole, disprove the presence of anti-Manichaean sentiments in *Doctr. Addai*.[36] Moreover, the independent existence of the name Addai does not mean that Christians in Edessa *could not have* used the name as a critique or revision of Manichaean claims. In Drijvers' assessment, the name Addai is a symbolic critique of Manichaeans in the city: it was the pro-Nicene Addai, not a disciple of Mani, who converted the king of Edessa. Only the followers of Addai may be called the true "Christians" of the city. Even if Addai is an older name in Christian tradition, the symbolism could still be relevant.

The evidence from the text thus suggests a number of important contextual factors. First, the form of *Doctr. Addai* that has survived must date to a time after Egeria, who knew of the insertion of the promise of Jesus, but did not know the name Addai. Second, the theological profile of the narrative suggests that it is a product of the crystallization of Nicene trinitarian doctrine in Edessa. Third, *Doctr. Addai*'s overt and symbolic, intra- and inter-Christian attacks on "other" religious groups in the city suggest a setting of religious competition within the city, with different groups vying for political and ideological prominence and primacy. Based on these factors, several scholars have suggested a date for the final form of *Doctr. Addai* in the early fifth century, most likely during the tenure of Bishop Rabbula (r. 411–435).[37]

The bishopric of Rabbula was a turbulent one in many respects. To Rabbula are attributed the reformation of the Edessene monastic and priestly orders, as well as the brutal suppression of "non-Christian" (non-Nicene) religious groups in the city.[38] Probably more famously, Rabbula is remembered as a strong supporter of Cyril of Alexandria at the beginning of the fifth-century christological controversies. Rabbula was at odds with other Christian factions in the city, among whom was the priest Hiba, whom Rabbula had exiled, but who would also succeed Rabbula as

---

36. Pedersen neither cites nor takes account of Desreumaux, "La figure du roi Abgar d'Édesse." This is important because Desreumaux includes examples from *Doctr. Addai* not addressed by Drijvers.

37. Griffith, "Doctrina Addai," 288–89; and Saint-Laurent, *Missionary Stories*, 36–55.

38. See Phenix and Horn, *Rabbula Corpus*; and Harvey, "Rabbula of Edessa."

bishop.[39] The first half of the fifth century was an eventful period in Edessa's history, to put it mildly. It was a period in which the Christians of Edessa were working to solidify their identity—a period into which *Doctr. Addai* fits quite nicely.

There are some challenges with the connections between *Doctr. Addai* and Rabbula. Griffith identifies "miaphysite" tendencies in the text, such as statements reflecting the views later espoused by the opponents of the council of Chalcedon (451 CE).[40] This implies that *Doctr. Addai* was composed at Rabbula's instigation (see the notes in the translation for such possible tendencies). While the language of "nature" and divinity could indicate a "miaphysite" bias, such a label may be anachronistic for a narrative developing in the early fifth century. Yet, Griffith writes: "To put it forward as the historical faith of Edessa suggests that the author of the *Doctrina Addai* was interested in propounding the Christological view associated with the teaching of Cyril of Alexandria (d. 444) in the context of the controversies of his own day."[41] While the label "miaphysite" may be anachronistic, it is at least possible that the author sought to align Edessa's history with the views of Cyril, views also shared by bishop Rabbula.

At the same time, other factors in *Doctr. Addai* may indicate it was written in *opposition* to Rabbula's regime, rather than in support of it. The prominence of the Edessene nobility in the narrative may indicate that certain families played a role in the formation of the story. The names of these nobles appear in numerous pre-Christian inscriptions in the environs of Edessa, suggesting they were genuine families with deep histories in the region.[42] The appearance of the family names was likely intended to promote the view, as Brock surmises, that "their pagan ancestors had converted to Christianity at a much earlier date than was in fact the case."[43] These nobles also may have been at odds with Rabbula, who worked to establish the Edessene episcopacy as the primary source of civic benefaction in the city,

---

39. See Doran, *Stewards of the Poor.*

40. Griffith, "Doctrina Addai," 288: "It would be difficult not to recognize in the phrase, 'God was crucified for all people,' [cf. ch. 36] a representation of the Christology of those whom their adversaries, after the time of the council of Chalcedon (451), would polemically label 'Monophysites.'"

41. Griffith, "Doctrina Addai," 288.

42. Brock, "Eusebius and Syriac Christianity," 228. See the notes on the various names in the translation.

43. Brock, "Eusebius and Syriac Christianity," 228.

rather than the nobility.[44] *Doctr. Addai* certifies that the noble families had been the supporters of the church from its beginnings, while Rabbula's regime was still fairly new. Kohlbacher recently hypothesized that *Doctr. Addai* was an "expression of local patriotism in Edessa and propagated, among other things, the long-standing privilege of some of Edessa's nobles."[45]

Another problem with associating *Doctr. Addai* directly with Rabbula is the promotion of the *Diatessaron. Doctr. Addai* specifically advocates for the reading of the *Diatessaron* in church (ch. 71). The Christians in Edessa had been reading the *Diatessaron* at least since the time of Ephrem, who also used it and wrote a commentary on it. Several of the Gospel quotations in *Doctr. Addai* appear to be Diatessaronic readings (see the commentary below). Rabbula, however, is remembered as discontinuing the use of the *Diatessaron* and specifically advocating for the use of the four-fold Gospel texts.[46] *Doctr. Addai* thus could be advocating for the continued use of the *Diatessaron* against Rabbula.

Finally, the approaches to the episcopacy of Edessa differ between *Doctr. Addai* and the fragments of information about Rabbula's legacy.[47] *Doctr. Addai* specifically denies that Addai or Abgar compelled people to believe by force (e.g., chs. 53, 67). The *Life of Rabbula*, by contrast, compares the bishop to Joshua bar Nun and Josiah:

> In (Rabbula's) obstinate conflicts with the host of [false] religions he was like Joshua bar Nun and especially [comparable] to the zeal of Josiah . . . For just as Joshua bar Nun and Josiah found the land of Canaan taken hold of by all the thickets of paganism, thus he also found the whole land of the house of the Edessenes entirely overgrown in the thickets of sin." (*Vit. Rab.* 40; trans. from Phenix and Horn, *Rabbula Corpus*, 59)

The writer goes on to mention the followers of Bardaisan in particular. *Doctr. Addai* may have been intended to contrast Rabbula's brutal suppression of other religious movements in the city in favor of Addai's gentle approach of instruction.

---

44. Phenix and Horn, *Rabbula Corpus*, lvi–lvii. The literature on Rabbula contains differing opinions about the Bishop's attitude toward the poor and civic benefaction in general. See Doran, *Stewards of the Poor*, 11–15.

45. Kohlbacher, "Rabbula *in* Edessa," 237; trans. from Phenix and Horn, *Rabbula Corpus*, lvi.

46. Phenix and Horn, *Rabbula Corpus*, lvi, 112–113.

47. On the challenges of reconstructing the history surrounding Rabbula, see Blum, *Rabbula von Edessa*; Doran, *Stewards of the Poor*; Phenix and Horn, *Rabbula Corpus*.

Doctr. Addai also claims that Addai built a church in the city (ch. 66) along with other churches, both within its walls (ch. 72) and in surrounding villages and cities (ch. 77). By contrast, Rabbula was remembered in some texts as being adamantly opposed to building projects and disdained the use of church funds for anything other than helping the poor (e.g., *Vit. Rab.*). Phenix and Horn suggest, "this is perhaps to show his independence from the system of patronage by which the wealthy controlled the church."[48] The wealthy nobility, who likely served in such patronage roles, play an important role throughout *Doctr. Addai* and are even portrayed as direct successors of Addai (chs. 65–66). Phenix and Horn conclude:

> [T]he *Doctrina Addai* uses the Abgar legend in order to demonstrate that Rabbula was an innovator, a rogue bishop who had nullified the tradition established with Edessa's first Christian king, a king moreover who had been in direct correspondence with Jesus himself and who received an icon touched by Christ's body, thus trumping any line of authority leading through an apostolic succession.[49]

The final form of *Doctr. Addai* thus appears to date to the tenure of Rabbula as bishop, but there is some debate about whether the narrative as we have it was reworked at Rabbula's instigation, or to counter Rabbula's approach to the episcopacy of Edessa. Either way, we may be certain that *Doctr. Addai* "is a text in which Edessa's 'Orthodox' Christians straighten, clean, and revise their representations of their Christian history in order to harmonize their foundation narrative with the orthodoxy that their bishops . . . claim before other bishops in the Roman Empire."[50]

Use of Scripture

Doctr. Addai makes a number of allusions to Hebrew Scripture, the canonical New Testament, and non-canonical scripture. In his major teaching section (chs. 36–61), Addai mentions the Prophets multiple times (cf. chs. 38, 40, 42, 52, 58). In ch. 67, the Jews search the Law and the Prophets based on Addai's testimony and many are persuaded and convert. Most significantly,

48. Phenix and Horn, *Rabbula Corpus*, lvii.

49. Phenix and Horn, *Rabbula Corpus*, lvii–lviii.

50. Saint-Laurent (*Missionary Stories*, 48) is convinced that *Doctr. Addai* was written at Rabbula's instigation, but her understanding of the purposes and efficacy of the narrative are conclusive even if it was written in opposition to Rabbula.

Doctr. Addai witnesses to the emergence of a notion of scripture advocated by the pro-Nicene, Palūtian faction responsible for the narrative's composition. After the initial success of Addai's preaching, the new believers dedicate themselves to the reading in the "Old Covenant and the New, and in the Prophets and in the Acts of the Apostles, meditating on them daily" (ch. 68). The distinctions between these works are not entirely clear, but the "Old Covenant" (*dyatāyqā ʿatayqtā*) here seems to refer to the Torah, as it is distinguished from the Prophets (*nbye*). Likewise, the "New Covenant" (*ḥadthā*) probably refers specifically to the Gospels, as distinguished from the "Acts of the Apostles" (*suʿrānayhun dašliḥe*).[51] This may be confirmed by Addai's later reference to these same scriptures in his final testament, that the people should continue to read "the Law and the Prophets and the Gospel" (ch. 88).

Yet, in another part of the narrative, the storyteller refers to the reading of "the Old Covenant, and the New of the *Diatessaron*" (*dyatāyqā ʿatayqtā wḥadthā ddyatesarun*) (ch. 71). Some scholars have suggested that one of these terms was actually an interpolation into the narrative based on disputes over the continued use of Tatian's popular harmony of the four canonical Gospels.[52] It is not unthinkable that the pro-Nicene Palūtians would have supported the use of the *Diatessaron*, given that Ephrem, a major proponent of their group, wrote a commentary on the *Diatessaron* and evidently supported its continued use.[53] The mention of it here promotes the idea that the *Diatessaron* is the *original* Gospel text used by the *original* church of Edessa, founded by Addai. The mention of the *Diatessaron*—whether it is an interpolation or not—is therefore intended for propagandistic purposes.

An analysis of the various individual Gospel quotations in *Doctr. Addai* cannot confirm the direct use of the *Diatessaron*.[54] Some of them appear

51. See the comments on ch. 68 for these titles.

52. Burkitt (*Evangelion da-Mepharreshe*, 2:174) argues that the term "new" was interpolated; Vööbus (*History of the Gospel Text in Syriac*, 13 n. 5) says the interpolated word was "*Diatessaron*." On the popularity of the *Diatessaron* in Syrian churches, see Brock, *Bible in the Syriac Tradition*, 33–34.

53. See McCarthy, *Saint Ephrem's Commentary*; and Leloir, *Commentaire de l'Évangile Concordant*.

54. The reconstruction of Diatessaronic readings is complicated. Individual quotations can almost never be undoubtedly identified as coming from the *Diatessaron*. On the challenges, see Barker, "Narrative Chronology"; see also the essays in Crawford and Zola, *Gospel of Tatian*.

to match the rendering of the Old Syriac translation, which was probably made after the *Diatessaron*.[55] At the same time, the sequence of the quotations occasionally follows the sequencing of the Diatessaron known from Ephrem's commentary. It is plausible, therefore, that some Gospel quotations in *Doctr. Addai* do indeed come from the *Diatessaron*.[56]

Manuscripts and Transmission

Doctr. Addai is extant exclusively in Syriac. There are four principal witnesses:[57]

> A: St. Petersburg, National Library of Russia, Siriyskaya novaya seria 4, fols. 1v–33r (5th/6th cent.); entire text
>
> B: London, British Library, Add. 14644, fols. 1–9 (5th cent.); chs. 41–47, 54–81, 92–104
>
> C: London, British Library, Add. 14645, fols. 32 and 33 (5th cent.); chs. 9–15, 20–24
>
> D: London, British Library, Add. 14535, fols. 1r–13r (9th cent.); chs. 36–39

The only surviving complete version of the text is found in the fifth/sixth-century St. Petersburg manuscript.[58] The contents of the manuscript are entirely apocrypha/hagiography:

1. *Doctrine of Addai*

2. *Preaching of Simon Cephas in the City of Rome*[59]

3. *History of John*[60]

---

55. Brock, *Bible in the Syriac Tradition*, 33.

56. See Desreumaux, "Neue Testament in der *Doctrina Addai*, 247–48.

57. One additional, unpublished manuscript—Cambridge Mass., Harvard Houghton Library, Syr. 93, fol. 58r (ca. 700)—contains a portion of ch. 90. Other unevaluated manuscripts are listed on the e-Clavis web site: https://www.nasscal.com/e-clavis-christian-apocrypha/doctrine-of-addai/. The text is often confused in catalog listings with the *Teaching of the Apostles* (see Cureton, *Ancient Syriac Documents*, 24–35 [text, Syriac numbering], 24–35 [English trans.]) which sometimes goes by the name "Teaching of Addai."

58. See Wright, "Syriac Manuscripts"; Pigulevskaya, "Katalog Siriyskikh"; and van Esbroeck, "Le manuscrit syriaque."

59. Introduction and translation in Walters, "Preaching."

60. See Lollar, *History of John*.

4. *Invention of the Cross* (Helena legend)[61]

5. *Invention of the Cross* (Judas Kyriakos legend)[62]

6. *Seven Sleepers of Ephesus*

7. *Life of Gregory Thaumaturgus*

8. *Life of Basil*

The pages containing *Doctr. Addai* were photographed and published by E.H. Meshtcherskaya in 1984.[63] The manuscript is in a clear Estrangelā script in two columns. The title given on the first folio is "A book/collection of the history of the holy ancestors." This is an interesting title in that the scribe of the manuscript appears to understand this collection of stories as constituting "history" in some form. The collection is even more interesting when compared to manuscript B in which a large portion of *Doctr. Addai* has survived. The overlap in content is striking:

<table>
<tr><td align="center">NLR Syr. 4</td><td align="center">BL Add. 14644</td></tr>
<tr><td>1. Doctr. Addai</td><td>1. Doctr. Addai</td></tr>
<tr><td>2. Pre. Pet. Rome</td><td>2. Teaching of the Apostles</td></tr>
<tr><td>3. History of John</td><td>3. Pre. Pet. Rome</td></tr>
<tr><td>4. Invention of the Cross (Helena)</td><td>4. Invention of the Cross (Helena)</td></tr>
<tr><td>5. Invention of the Cross (Judas Kyriakos)</td><td>5. Invention of the Cross (Judas Kyriakos)</td></tr>
<tr><td>6. Seven Sleepers of Ephesus</td><td>6. Life of Abraham of Qidun</td></tr>
<tr><td>7. Life of Gregory Thaumaturgus</td><td>7. Martyrdom of James Intercisus</td></tr>
<tr><td>8. Life of Basil</td><td>8. Life of Julien Sabas</td></tr>
<tr><td></td><td>9. Martyrdom of St. Sophia</td></tr>
<tr><td></td><td>10. Martyrdom of Sharbel</td></tr>
<tr><td></td><td>11. Life and Miracles of Cosmas and Damien</td></tr>
<tr><td></td><td>12. History of the Man of God</td></tr>
</table>

Not only do the two manuscripts share many of the same works, they share them in the same order. Much like the St. Petersburg manuscript (A), BL Add. 14644 (B) is a compendium of apocrypha and hagiography. In particular, both manuscripts share the thematic interest of the three distinct narratives of finding the True Cross (Protonike in *Doctr. Addai*, along with Helena and Judas Kyriakos). Moreover, B is intricately organized in a more-or-less chronological order, beginning with Addai coming to Edessa in the

61. See Drijvers, *Helena Augusta*.
62. See Drijvers and Drijvers, *Finding of the True Cross*.
63. Meshtcherskaya, *Legenda ob Avgare*, 119–84.

first century, continuing with the apostles (highlighting Peter in Rome), moving to the finding of the cross in Jerusalem two more times, then drawing attention to local Syrian martyrs like Abraham (purportedly in the 350s CE) and Sharbel (purportedly during the reign of Trajan, or perhaps Decius), and culminating with the story of the Man of God in the time of Rabbula. In effect, this compendium appears to be an attempt at chronicling the history of Christianity in Edessa using various apocryphal and hagiographical narratives. There are clear connections between the texts in the manuscript and they were probably edited to appear more seamless.

These two manuscripts may be further compared with manuscript C: BL Add. 14654. Cureton dated this manuscript "certainly not later than the beginning of the fifth century,"[64] though Wright was more cautious in assigning it to the fifth or sixth century. What is clear is that the contents are, much like the previous manuscripts, almost entirely apocrypha/hagiography:

1. Martyrdom of Acepsimas, Joseph, and Aitalāhā; Mīles, Abrūsīm, and Sīnī; Zebinā; Šabor, Isaac, M'anā, Abraham, and Simeon; Bademā; Šahdŏst; Barḥabbešabba; Tharbu, her sister, and her servant; 111 men and 9 women; Eleutherius, his mother, and the prefect Korbor; Lucius, Thyrsus, and Kallinus; Krescens(?); Alexander and Theodulus (all of these are very fragmentary)

2. *Doctr. Addai* chs. 20–24 (Protonike story)

3. *Doctr. Addai* chs. 9–15

4. Selections attributed to Ephrem: Discourse on Simon the Pharisee and the sinful woman from Luke 7; discourse on St. Simeon; five discourses on the fear of God

Evaluation of these three manuscripts leads to several observations about the use of *Doctr. Addai* in Edessa. First, there appears to be a correlation between the early period of Syriac literary activity and the copying/editing of apocryphal and hagiographical narratives. *Doctr. Addai* figures prominently in this period. Second, the arrangements of these stories in the manuscripts suggest that the editors were interested in them as chronicles for the early history of Edessa. This may be due to the fact that some of the stories—including *Doctr. Addai* and the *Martyrdom of Sharbel*—are said to have been found in the city's archives. The use of these texts in this way

64. Cureton, *Ancient Syriac Documents*, 147.

demands reconsideration of how late-antique Syriac Christians viewed the taxonomies of texts. For many of them, these narratives held both authority and credibility. Finally, *Doctr. Addai* in particular was received by these editors and scribes as a legitimate account of the coming of Christianity to Edessa, on par with other stories about apostles and martyrs.

The last witness, manuscript D (BL Add. 14535) from the ninth century, is different from the other manuscripts in that it contains a much more diverse grouping of texts.[65] In this instance, portions of *Doctr. Addai* (chs. 36–39; part of Addai's instruction to the Edessenes) are placed within a collection aimed at refuting dyophysite Christology, as the manuscript itself attests.[66] The authorities gathered in this collection to refute the "Nestorians" include:

1. *Doctr. Addai* (chs. 36–39)	16. Felix of Rome
2. Alexander of Alexandria	17. Gelasius of Antioch
3. Ambrose of Milan	18. George the Monk
4. Amphilocius of Iconium	19. Gregory Nazianzan
5. Anastasius of Antioch	20. Gregory of Nyssa
6. Athanasius	21. Helenus of Tarsus
7. Basil	22. Emperor Heraclius
8. John Chrysostom	23. Ignatius of Antioch
9. Cyril of Alexandria	24. Isaac of Antioch
10. Cyril of Jerusalem	25. Jacob of Batnae
11. Dionysius the Areopagite	26. Julius of Rome
12. Dionysius of Alexandria	27. Emperor Justinian
13. Ephrem the Syrian	28. Mennas of Constantinople
14. Epiphanius	29. Simeon Stylites the younger
15. Eustathius of Antioch	30. Vigilius of Rome

By the ninth century, then, *Doctr. Addai* was understood in some circles as a treatise defensive of the miaphysite christological position. Such an understanding fits with the context explored above with regard to the early fifth-century debates in Edessa involving bishop Rabbula. The inclusion of portions of Addai's teaching in a collection designed to refute dyophysite Christology adds to the notion that some Syriac Christians viewed *Doctr. Addai* as an authoritative narrative of the origins of Christianity in Mesopotamia. Addai's teachings were understood as legitimate enough to use in defense of miaphysitism.

65. Wright, *Catalogue*, 2:796–98.

66. Wright (*Catalogue*, 2:796) describes the collection as, "A treatise against the Nestorians, compiled by a Monophysite, of which the first five chapters are either lost or imperfect."

The different Syriac witnesses to *Doctr. Addai* also complicate the understanding of the form of the text. *Doctr. Addai* traditionally is understood to have survived completely only in manuscript A. This is certainly the longest form of the narrative, but we must consider the composite nature of the story. *Doctr. Addai* is comprised of several episodes, some of which likely originated independently and were edited into the larger composite form of the text. This is especially true of the letters of Abgar and Jesus.[67]

Other parts may be singled out as well. The legend of Protonike's finding of the True Cross likely originated independently of *Doctr. Addai* and was grafted into the story.[68] Significantly, this addition only appears to be true in manuscript A, the St. Petersburg text, whereas in B the Protonike legend may have appeared as a separate narrative. Due to damage to the beginning of the manuscript, *Doctr. Addai* starts at ch. 41 but the colophon on fols. 92v–93r describes the first several texts as "of king Abgar and the teaching of the Apostle Addai, and the finding of the Cross, and the finding of the Cross a second time, and the martyrdom of blessed bishop Kyriakos." Given that the colophon ends with the statement that the texts in the manuscript number 14, it would appear that "of king Abgar and the teaching of the Apostle Addai, and the finding of the Cross" are three separate texts. It may be significant also that manuscript C contains a fragment of the Protonike story on one folio and a fragment from what is titled the *Doctrine of Addai* on another—there is no way of knowing if these are witnesses to one text or two. Some scholars have suggested that Abgar's letters to Narseh and Tiberius (chs. 73–75) are external documents edited into *Doctr. Addai*.[69] Consequently, surviving copies of these individual narratives or letters may not necessarily constitute witnesses to *Doctr. Addai*. Moreover, given that none of the manuscripts preserves the exact same text as another, caution is warranted when speaking of an "original" text of *Doctr. Addai*. The story of Edessa's conversion developed and evolved in a fluid manner, and it may be best to avoid reference to an original, stable text.

---

67. It is interesting to note the differences between *Doctr. Addai* and the Syriac translation of Eusebius's *Ecclesiastical History*, which survives in a manuscript dated to 462 CE. I have included a translation of the Greek version of the letters in the appendices below. Despite an existing Syriac version of the letters in *Doctr. Addai*, the Syriac translation of Eusebius strictly adheres to the Greek version.

68. This point is argued definitively by Drijvers and Drijvers, *Finding of the True Cross*. The Protonike story circulated independently in several manuscripts.

69. Ramelli, "Possible Historical Traces."

The manuscripts of *Doctr. Addai* are thus quite diverse and show that a) the story was popular and regarded as both credible and authoritative, serving as a foundation myth for Christianity in the East; b) much like other apocryphal stories (e.g., the *Acts of Paul*), *Doctr. Addai* was often transmitted in distinct episodes, such as the letters of Abgar and Jesus and the Protonike legend; c) *Doctr. Addai* was considered authoritative enough that it was included by scribes in collections describing the history of Christianity in Edessa, but also in collections defending particular christological positions. Over time, other narratives would develop, such as the *Acts of Mār Māri*, that would integrate their own storylines into the mythical framework established by *Doctr. Addai*.

Witnesses and Diffusion

The mention of the letters of Abgar and Jesus by Eusebius undoubtedly contributed to their dissemination and popularity throughout the Mediterranean world and in multiple languages. In 384 CE, Egeria mentions her own version of the letters back in Spain, which evidently contained differences from the letters that were read to her by Bishop Eulogius in Edessa (see item 2 in Appendix A for Egeria's comments). Within a few decades of Eusebius's publication of his history, the letters of Abgar and Jesus were even being inscribed on city walls and gates. The inscriptional evidence is mostly confined to Syria and Asia Minor:[70]

> Alkat-Hadji-Kevi (Pontus) (4th cent.)
> Gurdja (Çorum) (4th cent.)
> Edessa (4th cent.)
> Philippi (5th cent.)
> Ephesus (5th cent.)
> Ankara (5th cent.)

Beyond inscriptions, the Abgar legend and *Doctr. Addai* specifically are referenced in various Greek authors.[71] The Abgar/Jesus correspondence is found in three Greek papyri (see Appendix A); Evagrius Scholasticus mentions the letters (*Hist. eccl.* 4.27); the *Acts of Thaddaeus* (seventh century) presents an alternative combination of the Abgar/Jesus correspondence

---

70. Introductions and translations of each of the inscriptions may be found in Appendix A.

71. See Saint-Laurent, *Missionary Stories*, 49–53.

and the coming of an apostle (in this case Thaddaeus) to Edessa; John of Damascus mentions a story close to the one in *Acts Thad.* in his *On the Orthodox Faith (De Fide Orthodoxa)*; and the *Story of the Image of Edessa,* an account of the arrival of the Image of Christ in Constantinople, contains details found also in *Doctr. Addai,* that is, that the image of Christ was a painting rather than an imprint of Jesus' face.[72]

The Abgar/Jesus correspondence—whether directly or indirectly, via *Doctr. Addai*—had an impact on a range of additional Syriac texts. Portions of the tradition are incorporated into the *Six-Books Dormition of Mary*[73] (and in turn the collected texts on Mary that make up the East Syriac *History of the Virgin*)[74] and the Syriac version of the *Legend of the Thirty Silver Pieces.*[75] In *Teach. Apos.* 6:9, Addai is named as the member of the seventy-two who evangelized Edessa and neighboring cities. And he appears as first of the seventy-two in the List of Apostles and Disciples attributed to Irenaeus. The author reports that "Addai preached in Edessa and Mesopotamia. He was a native of Paneas in the days of Abgar. And when he was in Sophene, Sawrus son of Abgar sent to kill him and his disciple-son in the citadel of Agel."[76] The same information is provided in the apostolic list in Solomon of Basra's *Book of the Bee* (49) along with a mention of the murder of Aggai by Abgar's son (cf. *Doctr. Addai* 100–101), who is said to have also killed Thaddaeus when he came to Edessa after Aggai's death.[77]

Doctr. Addai was translated into Armenian as early as the fifth century, though the extant manuscript evidence is rather late.[78] The Armenian

72. Greek text and German translation in Illert, *Doctrina Addai,* 260–311; new English translation in Hardy, "Story."

73. See Wright, "Departure of My Lady Mary," 134 (English trans.). Mention is made here of King Abgar sending a letter to Tiberius blaming the Jews for the death of Jesus (cf. chs. 74–75).

74. Budge, *History of the Blessed Virgin Mary,* 2:100–101 (English trans.)

75. English translation in Burke and Céplö, "Legend." The Syriac version of the legend is incorporated also in Solomon of Basra, *Bk. Bee* 44. Abgar is introduced in the text when the Magi, who carry the silver pieces, pass through Edessa. They forget the coins at a well and merchants use them to buy the seamless robe, which had been given to shepherds by an angel. King Abgar acquires both the coins and the robe and sends them to Jesus in return for his cure.

76. See van Esbroeck, "Neuf listes d'apôtres orientales," 163–66 (Syriac edition), 116–18 (French trans.).

77. English translation in Budge, *Book of the Bee,* 109.

78. Alichan, *Labubneay* (text); Alichan, *Lettre d'Abgar* (French trans.); Tchérakian, *Ankanon girkʿ aṟakʿelakankʿ,* 453–63 (text of two portions); Leloir, *Écrits apocryphes sur*

church was established quite early and set about translating many texts from the Syriac churches. The story of Christianity coming to Syria was adopted as the basis for the story of Christianity coming to Armenia as well.[79] As a result, the story of Abgar and his famous correspondence with Jesus "establishes a connection between the Church of Edessa and that of Armenia, thereby emphasising older Armenian Christianity's kinship with the Christianity of Osrhoene."[80]

In North Africa the correspondence between Abgar and Jesus is preserved in Coptic on wooden tablets, amulets, apotropaic inscriptions, and papyri.[81] These traces of the legend attest to the lasting influence and popularity of the epistles. In particular, the Coptic evidence confirms in several instances the use of the letters for apotropaic purposes among Christians in the region. Unlike the Armenians, the Coptic Christians appear to have been less interested in the extended form of the story, despite the possible presence of miaphysite themes in the narrative that could have served as a source against their detractors (as it did for their fellow Syrian Orthodox miaphysites).

Further south, the Ethiopian church also adapted the Abgar legend. It survives in multiple Ge'ez (Ethiopic) manuscripts, only two of which have been edited.[82] Desreumaux suggests that the Ge'ez version of the Abgar legend was copied via an Arabic medium, which is highly plausible, since Arabic often served as a medium for the transmission of texts from other languages into Ethiopic. There is some evidence of the legend in Arabic,

---

les apôtres, 2:687–704 (French trans. of Tchérakian's edition); and Langlois, *Collection*, 1:317–25 (French trans. based on a Paris manuscript). Portions of the text are inserted also in the *History of the Armenians* (2.26–36) by Moses of Khoren; see Carrière, *La légende d'Abgar*, 357–414; and Langlois, *Collection*, 1:326–31 (French trans.). It should be noted that the Armenian translator names the Apostle "Thaddaeus" as in the tradition of Eusebius. The text edited by Outtier ("Une forme enrichie de la Légende d'Abgar"), however, uses Addai and incorporates the *Legend of the Thirty Silver Pieces* (the elements of the Abgar story in the *Legend* forming a natural attraction).

79. Calzolari, "Réécriture des textes apocryphes en arménien." In the Armenian translation, Thaddaeus travels as a missionary throughout Mesopotamia and eventually brings Christianity to Armenia.

80. Calzolari, "Apostle Thaddaeus," 32.

81. Giverson, "Sahidic Version"; Blok, "Die koptischen Abgarbriefe"; Given, "Utility and Variance"; and Given, "Incipits Amulet."

82. The two manuscripts were translated into French by Robert Beylot and included in Desreumaux, *Histoire*, 147–52. The translation is based on the edition by Haile, "Legend of Abgar."

though this is primarily manifested by the letters of Abgar and Jesus and the legend concerning the Image of Christ.[83] That said, traces of the legend are found in the *Acts of Peter by Clement*[84] and the *Book of the Rolls*,[85] so the legend was at least known in Christian Arabic circles even if it did not circulate as an independent narrative. The extensive evidence for the Abgar legend in Syriac and Coptic suggests at least the possibility that the Ge'ez version is based on either of those languages. More work is needed on these versions to determine the modes of transmission more precisely.

Translation

Doctr. Addai has been translated into several modern languages, including English, French, German, Spanish, Italian, Russian, and even modern Syriac.[86] The first modern translation appeared in the nineteenth century by the British scholar George Phillips. His translation of manuscript A was followed by another English translation of B by William Cureton. In 1981, George Howard combined the two texts in an updated edition with English translation. Around the same time, Meshtcherskaya's study of the text in Russian appeared. Then, in 1990, Alain Desreumaux published his thorough study of the text, along with a French translation. These translations follow the "complete" text of *Doctr. Addai* from manuscript A. The present translation also takes A as its basis and includes notes and variants from other manuscripts. The translation technique used here is that of a dynamic equivalency to the Syriac. At times, I have adopted a smoother, idiomatic translation for the purposes of delivering a more readable English translation. In some instances, I have provided justification for my renderings of difficult Syriac expressions in the notes.

Following the format of Martin Illert's German edition (which also provides the most recent full modern translation), I have opted to include

83. Graf, *Geschichte der Christlichen Arabischen Literatur*, 1:237–38; and Gottheil, "Arabic Version."

84. Budge, *Contendings*, 1:382–435 (Ethiopic text), 2:466–526 (English translation).

85. Images of the Garšūnī text and partial translation in Mingana, "Apocalypse of Peter"; for background on the text, see Roggema, "Biblical Exegesis."

86. English: Phillips, *Doctrine of Addai*; Cureton, *Ancient Syriac Documents*; Howard, *Teaching of Addai*; Walters, "Doctrine of Addai"; French: Desreumaux, *Histoire*; German: Illert, *Doctrina Addai*; Spanish: González Núñez, *La Leyenda*; Italian: Casadei, *Didascalia di Addai*; Russian: Meshtcherskaya, *Legenda ob Avgare*; Modern Syriac: Oez, *I Malfonuto dAday u Şliḥo*.

several other translations in the Appendices, including Eusebius's Greek version of the Abgar/Jesus correspondence and Thaddaeus's arrival at Edessa, Egeria's account of her time in Edessa, the opening section of *Acts Thad.*, the opening section of *Acts Māri*, as well as a translation of each of the Greek inscriptions of the Abgar/Jesus correspondence. I have included these translations to give the reader a fuller view of the development and transmission of the legend of Abgar. Unlike Illert, I do not include legends concerning the Mandylion and the Image of Christ. The legend of the Image of Christ is rooted in the Abgar/Jesus correspondence, but has a separate and complex history of transmission. Therefore, while I do include a portion of *Acts Thad.*—which is an important text in the history of the Image of Christ—it covers only the epistolary correspondence for the purposes of showing the development of the letters themselves.

For the sake of clarity, I have adopted Alain Desreumaux's division of the chapters. This is the first English translation of *Doctr. Addai* to use these chapter divisions (they are used by both Illert and Núñez in their German and Spanish editions). The versification is my own and is based on my sense of the Syriac clauses—some of which are not always clear. The section divisions are based in part on Desreumaux's edition as well as on Griffith's sense of how the narrative is organized.[87] The complete version of the text as it appears in A is arranged by moments: the Abgar/Jesus correspondence; Addai's arrival at Edessa; Addai's conversion of Abgar; Addai's preaching to the citizens of Edessa; Addai's instructions for the church; and happenings after Addai's death.

The translation of certain terms deserves some comment. The term *mšiḥā*, can be translated as either "messiah" or "Christ"; previous translations have frequently used "messiah," but, given the Christian origins of the text, "Christ" is more appropriate. The phrase "hand of the priesthood" (*ʾaydā dkānūthā*), which refers to ordination, I have left literal, but in a few places only the term "hand" appears (see chs. 97 and 102). Proper names of people and places I have rendered literally and often left transliterated. I provide notations on these as much as possible. For Syriac transliterations I have relied on the current *SBL Handbook of Style*. For many other terms and phrases, see the notes in the translation.

---

87. Griffith, "Doctrina Addai."

1

The Doctrine of Addai the Apostle

Prologue

The letter[A] of King Abgar, son of King Ma'nu,[B] when he sent it to our Lord in Jerusalem, and when Addai the apostle came to him in Urhay[C]: that which he spoke in the gospel of his preaching, and those things which he spoke and commanded, as he departed from this world, to those who had the hand of the priesthood[D] from him.

A. *the letter*: the entire narrative of *Doctr. Addai* is constructed around the epistolary correspondence between Abgar and Jesus. The letters not only serve as a locus for the events surrounding Addai's coming to Edessa, they also provide an air of authenticity and verisimilitude to this account of Edessa's early Christian history. See also the mention of the archives below in ch. 103.

B. *King Ma'nu*: there were many Abgars and Ma'nus in the royal line of Edessa from about 133 BCE to the third century CE; this aids the writer in situating the mythic narrative in a historical past. See Wardle, "Abgarids of Edessa."

C. *Urhay*: the Syriac name for the city of Edessa (modern day Sanliurfa, Turkey). The ancient name was Adme. See Harrak, "Ancient Name of Edessa."

D. *hand of the priesthood*: Syr: *'īdā dkāhnūthā*. A typical phrase denoting ordination. The use here and throughout *Doctr. Addai* mirrors exactly the use in *Teach Apos*.

1 [1]In the three hundred and forty-third year of the reign of the Greeks,[A] during the reign of our lord Tiberius the Roman Caesar,[B] during the reign of King Abgar, son of King Ma'nu, in the month of October on the twelfth day, Abgar Ukkāmā[C] sent Māryāhb and Šmešgrām,[D] nobles and dignitaries of his kingdom, and along

A. *the reign of the Greeks*: Syriac Christian writers tended to retain the Seleucid calendar which started in 311 BCE. The date 343 thus refers to the year 31/32 CE. On the use of the Seleucid calendar by Syriac historians and hagiographers, see Debié, "Syriac Historiography." On the date of the correspondence, see *Chron. Zuq.* 95, which may have relied on *Doctr. Addai* as a source.

B. *Tiberius the Roman Caesar*: reigned from 14–37 CE. Based on the date given in the previous clause, the story is purportedly taking place right around the end of Jesus' life and ministry and near the end of Tiberius's reign. There may be some confusion about rulers in *Doctr. Addai*, as the storyteller later introduces Claudius as "Caesar" (16:2; 76:1) as well as Gaius (76:2), who would ultimately succeed Tiberius as emperor. See also the notes in those sections.

C. *Ukkāmā*: an appellation meaning "black," "tanned," or "burnt." Typically, this Abgar is identified as Abgar III, who reigned from 4 BCE to 7 CE, was briefly overthrown, and then regained power to rule from 13–50 CE. The appellation "black" may refer to skin tone, as was evidently common in reference to dark-skinned men among Arabs, but in at least one Greek tradition of the letters of Abgar and Jesus, the "blackness" refers to leprosy, which is thus identified as Abgar's illness for which he seeks healing from Jesus. See Desreumaux, *Histoire*, 127–28.

D. *Māryāhb and Šmešgrām*: Babylonian theophoric names, meaning "God has given" and "God has judged," respectively. The name Šmešgrām in particular has direct connections to the Babylonian deity Shamash, whose name appears in Syrian inscriptions, particularly in Palmyra. See Desreumaux, *Histoire*, 131. This name is evidently connected with a noble house in Edessa who will be among the first converts of Addai (see ch. 35). The name, along with several others, also appears in *Mart. Sharb.* and *Mart Bars.* (trans. in Cureton, *Ancient Syriac Documents*, 45, 63) and it can be found in inscriptions in Syria (see Drijvers, *Old-Syriac Inscriptions*, no. 28; Brock, "Eusebius," 228–29). In *Chron. Ed.*, Šmešgrām is one of the scribes who wrote about the events of the flood of 201 CE and the destruction of the Christian church (text in Guidi, *Chronica Minora I*, 3). Most importantly, perhaps, Šmešgrām appears as a friend of Bardaisan in *Bk. Laws.* Several names from this text are shared with *Doctr. Addai*, strengthening the connections between Abgar VIII the Great—at whose court Bardaisan appeared—and the "King Abgar" of the Abgar/Jesus correspondence. The use of these names in *Doctr. Addai* also introduces elements of interreligious polemic between the "Nicene" supporters behind *Doctr. Addai* and other Christian factions, such as Bardaisanites. By mentioning the same names as people involved with Bardaisan,

with them Ḥanan,[A] the faithful archivist, to the city called Eleutheropolis (in Aramaic Beth Gubrin)[B] to the honorable Sabinus,[C] son of Eustorgius, the procurator of our lord Caesar. [2]It was he who had charge over Syria, Phoenicia, Palestine, and all of the region of Mesopotamia. [3]They brought him letters concerning the affairs of the kingdom. [4]Upon reaching him, he received them with joy and honor and they remained in (the city)[D] twenty-five days. [5]He wrote for them a response to the letters and sent them to King Abgar.

2 [1]When they had gone forth from his presence, they departed and went on the road toward Jerusalem. [2]They saw many people coming from far and wide in order to see Christ, since rumor of the wonders of his extraordinary feats had gone forth into distant lands. [3]And seeing those people, Māryāhb, Šmešgrām, and Ḥanan the archivist also went with them to Jerusalem. [4]Upon entering Jerusalem, they saw Christ and rejoiced with the crowds

---

the storyteller tries to claim these people—whose names are embedded in Edessa's history—for his own narrative of Christianization of the city.

A. *Ḥanan*: the Greek text has Ananias (Eusebius, *Hist. eccl.* 1.13.9). Eusebius refers to Ananias as a *tachydromos* ("courier").

B. *Beth Gubrin*: lit: "House of Strong Men." Modern Beit Guvrin, Israel, located approximately 40 km southwest of Jerusalem. Josephus mentions this city being taken by Vespasian during the Jewish War (*J. W.* 4.8.1). Eleutheropolis ("City of the Free") was the Roman name given to the city by Septimius Severus in 200 CE. Based on the form of the name in Syriac, *Doctr. Addai* could not possibly date prior to the renaming of the city. The route is strange here as well. Coming from Edessa, the messengers would have had to pass by Jerusalem. The explanation seems to be that they wanted to check in with the procurator of the region before entering Jerusalem, as is made clearer in ch. 3, where Abgar himself cannot cross into the Roman empire without causing political trouble.

C. *Sabinus*: another blatant anachronism. Eusebius mentions a Sabinus who served under the emperor Maximian and transmitted the emperor's edict in 235 CE (*Hist. eccl.* 9.1.2–6). The Syriac writer uses the Greek word *epitropos* ("procurator") to describe Sabinus's position. See Desreumaux, *Histoire*, 131.

D. *(the city)*: the text has a feminine pronoun (*hė*). This would mean that the pronoun refers logically back to the city of Eleutheropolis. Phillips and Howard both take this as a masculine pronoun (*he*) referring to Sabinus and thus translate the passage as "they remained *with him* twenty-five days." Dots in Syriac are notoriously difficult to assess, especially in these early manuscripts.

who were following him. [5]They also saw the Jews,[A] who were standing in groups and plotting what they might do to him. [6]For they were distressed to see the great number of people who were believing in him.

[7]They were there in Jerusalem for ten days and Ḥanan the archivist wrote down everything he saw Christ doing, as well as everything else done by him there before they had come there. [8]Then they departed and came to Urhay. [9]When they entered before King Abgar, their lord who had sent them, they gave him the reply to the letters they had brought with them. [10]After the letters were read, they began to narrate to the king everything they had seen and everything Christ had done in Jerusalem; Ḥanan the archivist read before (Abgar) everything he had written and brought with him.[B]

3 [1]When King Abgar heard (these reports), he was dumbfounded and amazed, as were his nobles[C] who were standing before him. [2]Abgar said to them, "These powers are not of human beings but of God! For there is no one who can give life to the dead except God alone." [3]Then Abgar desired that he himself might cross over and go into Palestine and that he might see with his own eyes everything that Christ was doing. [4]But because he was

A. *the Jews*: "the Jews" serve as the primary antagonist in *Doctr. Addai*. In general, they are portrayed in a negative light, referred to as the "crucifiers" throughout the narrative. However, this portrait is somewhat inconsistent, given that Addai's first official convert happens to be the hospitable Jew Tobia, with whom Addai lives when he first comes to Edessa. See Desreumaux, *Histoire*, 134; Drijvers, "Jews and Christians at Edessa."

B. This report explains Abgar's statement that he has heard about Jesus' miracles (see the letter in ch. 4). But we hear nothing in the current chapter about Jesus' specific healings, which are the primary focus of Abgar's interest. We are made to assume that Ḥanan wrote down the details of such healings.

C. *his nobles*: the Edessene nobles play an integral part in *Doctr. Addai*. The same families who make up the Edessene nobility appear in several other texts related to Edessa's Christian past. Remarkably, these texts tend to appear together in the two manuscripts (A and B) in which *Doctr. Addai* appears. The link between these manuscripts suggests that the compilers and editors behind them had the backing of the nobility represented in these texts as the earliest supporters of and converts to Christianity. See Brock, "Eusebius," 228–29. On the manuscripts and their relationship, see van Esbroeck, "Le manuscrit syriaque," 210–19.

not able to cross over into the region of the Romans,[A] which was not his own, lest this affair invite bitter enmity, he wrote a letter and sent (it) to Christ via Ḥanan the archivist. [5]So (Ḥanan) went forth from Urhay on the fourteenth of Adar and entered Jerusalem on the twelfth of Nisan,[B] on the fourth day of the week. [6]He found Christ at the home of Gamaliel,[C] chief of the Jews.

The Letter of Abgar to Jesus Christ

4 [1]The letter was read to him, which was written as follows:[D]

A. *the region of the Romans*: Edessa was a part of the territory of Osrhoene, which had been created after the defeat of the Greek king Antiochus Sidetes in 130/129 BCE at the hands of the Parthians. Osrhoene enjoyed relative independence, had its own set of kings, and served as a buffer state between Rome and the Parthians until it became a Roman territory in 213 CE. During the Roman invasion of Parthia under Marcus Aurelius (163 CE) the king of Edessa was briefly replaced by a Parthian client who ruled until 165 CE and was eventually replaced by the Abgarid king, who declared Edessa/Osrhoene a "friend of Rome" on his coinage. See Millar, *Roman Near East*, 112–13.

B. *Adar*: = March; *Nisan* = April. By modern routes, Edessa is nearly 1,000 km from Jerusalem. No doubt it would have taken about a month to travel between the cities by foot. The travel time may have been known to the fifth-century storyteller of *Doctr. Addai*, since travelers and pilgrims likely made the trip between Edessa and Jerusalem. The pilgrim Egeria made this trip and her route can be traced (see Wilkinson, *Egeria's Travels*, 114). Egeria locates Edessa 25 staging-posts from Jerusalem (*Itin.* 17.2). Wilkinson estimates that if Egeria left Jerusalem on March 25 (after the Easter celebration), she could have arrived in Carrae (just southeast of Edessa) by April 23 (Wilkinson, *Egeria's Travels*, 29). The two timelines adhere close enough to render the time frame in *Doctr. Addai* quite plausible. The storyteller is also clearly interested in placing Ḥanan in Jerusalem with Jesus before Easter of 31 CE, the day before Jesus' death. See Desreumaux, *Histoire*, 56 n. 18.

C. *Gamaliel*: rescuer of the early Christians from execution in Acts 5:33–39. He was also the purported teacher of Paul (Acts 22:3). Nowhere in the Gospels does Jesus ever interact directly with Gamaliel, though Gamaliel does become involved in events at the tomb of Jesus in the Arabic-Ethiopic (originally Coptic) *Lament of the Virgin* and its sequel the *Martyrdom of Pilate*. For Arabic texts and English translations see Mingana in *Woodbrooke Studies* 2.

D. *which was written as follows*: we are expected to take this as a copy of Abgar's letter, which, according to Eusebius (*Hist. eccl.* 1.13.5) and according to the end of *Doctr. Addai* (ch. 103), was deposited in the royal archives of the city. The bishop of Edessa who gives Egeria a tour (probably Eulogius, who was bishop from 377–387 CE; see Devos, "La date du voyage," 165–94) reads

²"Abgar Ukkāmā to Jesus, the good physician who has appeared in the region of Jerusalem: greetings, my lord. ³I have heard about you and about your healing—that you do not heal with drugs and herbs.ᴬ Rather, it is by your word that you open (the eyes) of the blind, make the lame walk, cleanse lepers, and make the deaf hear. ⁴By your word you heal spirits, epileptics, and the tormented. You even raise the dead. ⁵When I heard about these great marvels that you are doing, I determined either that you are God who has descended from heaven and have performed these (wonders), or that you are a Son of God who does all of these things.ᴮ ⁶For this reason, I have written requesting that you come to me, since I revere you, and heal a certain disease I have, since I believe in you.ᶜ ⁷Moreover, I have heard that the Jews are murmuring against you, persecuting you, and are even seeking to crucify you; they are looking for a way to harm you.ᴰ ⁸I

Matt 11:5//
Luke 7:22

---

from these letters (and supplies her with copies of them), though Egeria says nothing about the archives (*Itin.* 19.19).

A. *you do not heal with drugs and herbs*: there is no direct reference to healings in the narrative prior to this, but we are made to assume that such healings were accounted for in Ḥanan's description of Jesus and his miracles. The idea of healing without medicine is popular in Syriac hagiography (see, e.g., *Mart. Nars.*). In the afterlife of the epistles of Abgar and Jesus, Abgar's letter becomes a source of apotropaic power for believers throughout the Mediterranean seeking healings. See Given, "Utility and Variance."

B. *I determined . . . these things*: a testimony of Abgar's belief without seeing, which Jesus highlights in his reply. As the narrative unfolds, after Addai comes to Edessa and preaches the gospel, it becomes clear that Jesus is to be reckoned as God. The christological make-up of *Doctr. Addai* predominantly features affirmations of Nicene Christology. It may contain some nascent forms of miaphysitism, which would become the primary confession of Edessa during the course of the fifth century. See the note, for example, in ch. 41.

C. *heal a certain disease . . . believe in you*: no version of the letter reveals the nature of the disease. This request for healing and Jesus' promise in his letter that it would come (see 5:5 below) became important elements in the preservation of the letters of Abgar and Jesus for apotropaic purposes. See Given, "Utility and Variance."

D. *they are looking for a way to harm you*: once again, "the Jews" take center stage as the antagonists of the narrative. There is an implied sense of urgency in Abgar's statement, since, within the broader scope of the narrative, Ḥanan is reading the letter to Jesus just prior to Jesus' arrest, trial, and execution at the hands of the Jews. We may detect some prophetic foreknowledge ascribed

have a small and beautiful city and it is sufficient for two to dwell in it in peace."

The Reply of Jesus Christ to King Abgar

5 ¹When Jesus had received the letter in the house of the high priest of the Jews, he said to Ḥanan the archivist, "Go and say to your lord who sent you to me:ᴬ

²Blessed are you who, though you have not seen me, have believed in me.ᴮ ³For it is written about me that those who see me will not believe in me, but those who do not see me will believe in me. ⁴Now, you have written to me to come to you. That for which $\quad$ John 20:29 I was sent here is now completed and I am about to ascend to my Father who sent me. ⁵But when I have ascended to him, I will send to you one of my disciples so that he might heal and cure whatever pain you have and that he might turn all who are with you toward eternal life. ⁶Now, for your city: may it be blessed and may no enemy ever again have authority over it."ᶜ

---

to Abgar in this instance. The timing of the letter's arrival is an invention of the author of *Doctr. Addai* and it is probable that he intended to bolster not only the verisimilitude of the narrative account, but also went through pains to show that Abgar, in his own way, attempted to intervene in the events surrounding Jesus' execution. See Desreumaux, *Histoire*, 56 n. 18.

A. *Go and say to your lord who sent you to me*: Jesus' reply is not portrayed as a letter written by his own hand; rather, we are to understand that Ḥanan took down Jesus' response by dictation. Egeria's testimony to this is somewhat mixed. She says that the bishop of Edessa told her "King Abgar wrote a letter to the Lord, and the Lord wrote back through Ananias the courier" (*Itin.* 19.8; my trans.). This statement agrees with *Doctr. Addai* in this regard, which suggests that the bishop already knew this version of the correspondence in 384. At the same time, in the rest of Egeria's account, Jesus' reply is referred to as "the Lord's letter" (*Itin.* 19.9; 19.17; 19.19; my trans.). Thus, despite the apparent *quid pro quo* that Jesus did not *technically* write the letter in his own hand, that this was *the Lord's* letter is evidently unquestioned.

B. *though you have not seen me, have believed in me*: an obvious reference to John 20:29. The significance of referring to this passage lies in the fact that it is (Judas) Thomas who will send Addai to Edessa in ch. 7. Clearly the statement, along with the follow-up "for it is written about me . . . ," are anachronistic as John's Gospel was not composed before the death of Jesus.

C. This final statement does not exist in the earliest Greek version of the text—that of Eusebius. It is, however, one of the most important statements in the history of the transmission of these letters (see Given, "Utility and

6 [1]So when Ḥanan the archivist saw that Jesus had spoken to him this way, and because he was the king's painter, he took up (paints) and painted the portrait of Jesus with choice pigments and brought it with him to his lord King Abgar.[A] [2]When King

---

Variance"). The statement is mentioned by the bishop who gives Egeria a tour of the city (*Itin.* 19.9), so the statement must have been added sometime between Eusebius's composition of *Hist. eccl.* and 384, when Egeria visited Edessa. It is highly plausible that the divine protection of Edessa was an idea imported to the city by refugees from Nisibis, who arrived in 363 after the fortress city was ceded to the Sassanian king Shapur II. Nisibis has a similar legend to the one told by the Edessene bishop that reportedly took place at the siege of Nisibis in 350 (see Theodoret, *Hist. eccl.* 2.30). The prestige of Nisibis was thus transferred onto Edessa by refugees so that, in Drijvers' words, "Edessa is presented as the true heir of Nisibis's glorious Christian past" ("Syriac Romance of Julian," 211). This is also the conclusion of Segal, *Edessa*, 75 (see also Lollar, *Sanctifying Myth*, 53–59). The word "enemy" here could refer to foreign occupation, as it was interpreted in many of the later versions of the correspondence, but it could also symbolically refer to *the* enemy, i.e., Satan, whose rule would be symbolically assumed due to the paganism in the city. Such an interpretation is attractive given the emphasis on ridding Edessa of "other" religious groups (including those Christian groups not considered "orthodox" by the storyteller). See Taylor, "Coming of Christianity," 72.

A. *painted the portrait of Jesus . . . King Abgar*: the earliest extant reference to the famous Mandylion portrait, purportedly housed in Edessa until its translation to Constantinople in 944 CE. Drijvers suggests that *Doctr. Addai* served as the catalyst for a new development of the tradition where Jesus instead imprinted his image onto a cloth with the result that the Mandylion was truly considered an *acheiropoietos*, or not made by human hands (cf. Drijvers, "Image of Edessa"). Later Eastern developments of the legend of the Mandylion include the *Life of Jacob of Galash* (6th cent.), Evagrius Scholasticus (6th cent.), the *Acts of Thaddaeus* (7th cent.), the *Acts of Mār Māri* (6th/7th cent.), the colophon of an eighth-century Melkite manuscript, John of Damascus *On the Orthodox Faith* (8th cent.), Theodore Abū Qurrah (800 CE), and the narration of the arrival of the Mandylion to Constantinople (944 CE) (see Saint-Laurent, *Missionary Stories*, 49–53). There is an icon of the Mandylion in the Monastery of St. Catherine at Mt. Sinai, probably created around the same time the Mandylion was translated to Constantinople (see Brock and Taylor, *Hidden Pearl*, 2:49; Brock, "Transformations," 46). Neither Eusebius nor Egeria mention the portrait of Christ and this has been taken to mean that it was a later interpolation, since the portrait plays a much greater role in Edessa's salvation in both Evagrius Scholasticus and in Procopius (cf. Mirkovic, *Prelude to Constantine*, 36). This would suggest that the Mandylion legend took on greater significance in the late sixth century and beyond. The theory of interpolation does not, however, fit with the manuscript evidence of *Doctr. Addai* itself, which attests to the existence of the legend by the mid

Abgar saw the portrait he received it with great joy and set it with great honor in one of the rooms of his palaces. ³And Ḥanan the archivist narrated to him everything he heard from Jesus, since his words had been written by him in books.ᴬ

7 ¹Now, after Christ had ascended into heaven, Judas Thomasᴮ sent to Abgar the apostle Addai,ᶜ who was one of the seventy-two apostles.ᴰ ²When Addai came to the city of Urhay he stayed in

Luke 10:1–12, 17–20

---

to late fifth century. More convincing is Drijvers' conclusion that the *Doctr. Addai* storyteller knew of an icon of Christ in Edessa and the story of its origins developed into the more elaborate forms we find in later texts. The whole notion of painting a portrait of a revered figure is reminiscent of Porphyry's mention of a secret portrait of his master Plotinus painted by one of Porphyry's fellow students (*Vit. Plot.* 1).

A. *since his words had been written by him in books*: that is, Ḥanan wrote down the words of Jesus. One would think such a document would constitute the status of a gospel, but nothing is mentioned of these written words again in the story. The focus now shifts to the arrival and preaching of Addai.

B. The role of Judas Thomas here is consistent with his role in Eusebius's account, though Eusebius uses the name Thaddaeus instead of Addai. In both accounts, the disciple sent by Thomas is one of the seventy-two from Luke 10, though a Thaddaeus is listed as one of the Twelve in Mark and Matthew. From Egeria's testimony, she understood Thomas to have been the one sent to Edessa and she makes no mention of Addai. Palmer ("King Abgar") suggests that two different versions of the legend existed, one in which Thomas was sent and one in which Thomas sent another. Nathanael Andrade (*Journey of Christianity*, 54–60) has recently argued that the earliest layers of the *Acts of Thomas* traditions place Thomas in Parthia, rather than India. By the early fifth century, when *Doctr. Addai* came into its final form, Thomas's relics were said to be in Edessa (see Devos, "Égérie à Edesse") and he was clearly a venerated saint in the city (and the primary reason for Egeria's visit). The shift away from Thomas as the actual apostle to Edessa must have occurred sometime in the fourth century.

C. *Addai*: in Eusebius and the Greek tradition, he is called Thaddaeus. The name Addai probably was inserted in response to rival Manichaean claims about the origins of Christianity in Edessa. Mani had a disciple named Adda who also was said to have been sent to an Edessene king and converted him (see Drijvers, "Addai und Mani"; Desreumaux, "La figure du roi Abgar"; for the legends of Adda, disciple of Mani, see Gardner and Lieu, *Manichaean Texts*, 111–14).

D. *the seventy-two apostles*: Jesus commissions additional apostles in Luke 10:1–12, but the exact number is different in the manuscript traditions of Greek and Syriac. Most Greek manuscripts have seventy (א A C K L and M) as does the Old Syriac (Lewisian and Curetonian). A few Greek manuscripts (B P75 D), the Latin tradition, and the Philoxenian and Harklean

the house of Tobia Bar Tobia the Jew, who was from Palestine. [3]Then it was heard about him all over the city, so one of Abgar's nobles—his name was 'Abdu bar 'Abdu, one of the princes who sits in Abgar's council—entered (before Abgar) and told him about Addai: "Look: an emissary has come and stayed here, that one about whom Jesus sent to you (saying): 'I will send to you one of my disciples.'" [4]When Abgar heard these things, as well as the great miracles Addai was performing and the wonderous cures he was enacting, he resolved and concluded, "Truly this is he whom Jesus sent (saying), 'When I have ascended to heaven, I will send to you one of my disciples and he will heal your pain.'" [5]Then Abgar sent and called for Tobia saying to him, "I have heard that a powerful man has come and is staying in your house. Bring him to me. Perhaps a great hope of recovery will be found for me from him." [6]The next day, Tobia rose and led the apostle Addai and brought him to Abgar, though Addai himself knew full well that it was by the power of God that he was being sent to him.

8 [1]When Addai went up and entered before Abgar, while his nobles were standing around him, at (the moment of) his entrance before him, a wonderous vision appeared to Abgar from the face of Addai.[A] [2]The moment Abgar saw the vision, he fell down and bowed before Addai. [3]Great wonder captured all those who were standing near him, for they had not seen the vision that had appeared to Abgar. [4]Then Abgar said to Addai, "Truly you are a disciple of Jesus, that mighty one, the Son of God, the one who sent me (a message) that 'I am sending you one of my disciples for healing and for salvation.'"

Syriac traditions have seventy-two. *Hist. John* 13 refers to the "seventy-two" in the youth Menelaus's vision, but several lines later all the manuscripts have "seventy." In his commentary on the *Diatessaron*, Ephrem mentions that they went "two by two"—another disputed variant in the manuscript traditions of Luke. Ephrem's *Diatessaron* commentary matches the Harklean version in this case. Eusebius (*Hist. eccl.* 1.13.11) says Thaddaeus is one of the "seventy." The two main *Doctr. Addai* manuscripts both agree on seventy-two.

A. *wonderous vision . . . from the face of Addai*: transformations of appearance, especially of the face, are common. When Moses descends from Mt. Sinai in Exod 34:35, the Israelites can hardly bear to look on his face. John's face in *Hist. John* 14 is "like light" (trans. Lollar, *History of John*).

9 ¹Addai replied,[A] "Because from the first you have believed in the one who sent me to you, for that reason I have been sent to you. Again: since you believe in him everything you believe will happen for you through him." ²Abgar said to him, "I believe in him so much that I wish to lead my army myself against those Jews who crucified him and go forth and destroy them, but because that kingdom is of the Romans, I am impeded by a covenant of peace established by me with our lord Caesar Tiberius, as it was with my forefathers."[B] ³Addai replied, "The Lord has accomplished the will of his Father and after completing the will of his begetter, he was lifted up to his Father and sat down with him in glory, with whom he had been forever."[C] ⁴Abgar said to him, "Indeed, I believe in him and in his Father." ⁵Addai replied,

John 20:29

John 6:38

John 17:5

A. Here begins the fragment of C.

B. *as it was with my forefathers*: this is another anachronism, probably based on the periods of the Antonine or Severan dynasties. Rome became increasingly powerful in the region of northern Mesopotamia after the invasions of Parthia by Lucius Verus (r. 161–169 CE) and Septimius Severus (r. 193–211 CE). Any treaties with Rome would have likely occurred in these periods, when Edessa shifted allegiances between Rome and Parthia on a regular basis. *Chron. Zuq.* 123 says that, in 116 CE, King Ma'nu son of Ma'nu "crossed over into Roman territory," and this appears to occur in the context of several uprisings, particularly among the Jews in northern Egypt. The Chronicler does not say why Ma'nu crossed into Rome, nor does he clarify any consequences incurred by Edessa for doing so. Later, *Chron. Zuq.* 125 says that this Ma'nu "returned from the Roman land," so it may be that he was a client hostage, or perhaps he was in danger of being overthrown and sought refuge in Rome. Ma'nu would appear to be the father of Abgar VIII, the Great, who reigned from 177–212 CE and saw the end of Edessene independence. The mention of peace agreements between Edessa and Rome reflects the period of Abgar VIII more appropriately than that of Abgar V Ukkāmā.

C. *with whom he had been forever*: a reference to the preexistence of Christ. While this is a perfectly ordinary Nicene christological sentiment, it could also be read as an early miaphysite statement. Early proponents of a single-nature Christology advocated for a unity of Christ's divine and human natures. In his second letter to Nestorius of Constantinople, Cyril of Alexandria writes: "(Christ) did not depart from his divine status or cease to be born of the Father; he continued to be what he was, even in taking on flesh" (trans. from Norris, *Christological Controversy*, 134). In Edessa, bishop Rabbula became a supporter of Cyril. He wrote in his letter to Andrew of Samosata: "the separation of the natures troubles me much, especially [the separation] after the union" (trans. from Phenix and Horn, *Rabbula Corpus*, 147).

"Since you have believed in this way, I am setting my hand upon you in the name of the one in whom you have believed."

10 ¹In the moment that (Addai) set his hand upon (Abgar), he was healed of the pain of the disease which he had had for a long time. ²Abgar marveled and was astonished that, just as he had heard how Jesus had performed and healed, so also Addai healed in the name of Jesus without a drug of any kind. ³Also 'Abdu bar 'Abdu[A] had gout in his feet and brought his feet to him and Addai set his hand upon them and healed him and he no longer had gout. ⁴Also throughout the whole city (Addai) performed great healings and displayed astonishing feats.

11 ¹Abgar said to him, "Now everyone knows that you perform these wonders by the power of Jesus Christ. Look: we are astonished by your deeds! ²Therefore, I beg you, tell us of the coming of Christ, how it happened, about his glorious power, and about those wonders which we have heard he performed, those which you and the rest of your companions[B] saw."

12 ¹Addai said to him, "I will not rest from preaching this, for it is because of this that I was sent here, that I might speak and teach to everyone who, like you, is willing to believe. ²Assemble all the city to me tomorrow and I will sow the word of life into it by the preaching I will proclaim to you: about the coming of Christ, how it was; about his glorious power;[C] about why and how he sent him; his power and wonderous deeds, the glorious mysteries of his coming which he spoke in the world, and the accuracy of his preaching; ³how and for what reason he lowered himself and humbled his exalted divinity by means of the body[D] which he took; (how) he was crucified and went down to the grave and broke through that barrier which had never been broken through (before) and gave the dead life by his being killed.

Phil 2:6–8

A. *'Abdu bar 'Abdu*: lit. "servant." This character is mentioned throughout *Doctr. Addai* and is said to have been Abgar's majordomo in 14:2 (Syr. *trayānā dmalkuthe*, lit. "second of his kingdom").

B. *the rest of your companions*: C has "your fellow disciples."

C. *about his glorious power*: C omits this phrase.

D. *the body*: C has "humanity."

[4]He descended alone,[A] but ascended with many to his glorious Father, with whom he existed from everlasting in one exalted divinity."[B]

13 [1]Abgar ordered that silver and gold be given to Addai. [2]Addai replied, "How can we receive anything which is not ours?[C] Look: everything that is ours has been left to us just as we were commanded by the Lord not to have purses or wallets. [3]We were commanded to preach his gospel in all of creation, while bearing crosses on our shoulders—that whole of creation which was in an uproar and anguished at his crucifixion, which happened for the sake of the salvation of all humanity."

Matt 10:9–10// Luke 10:4

Mark 16:15; Matt 28:19; Acts 1:8

Matt 10:38, 16:24; Luke 9:23, 14:27

Matt 27:51

14 [1]Then he recounted before King Abgar and his nobles and princes, Augustina (Abgar's mother),[D] (and) Šalmath daughter of Meherdath (Abgar's wife),[E] the signs, wonders, and glorious

A. *he descended alone*: this phrase is reminiscent of the Apostles' Creed. Throughout his hymns, Ephrem the Syrian speaks often of Christ's descent into Sheol (see, e.g., *Cruc.* 8; *Nis.* 36; *Azym.* 3). Ephrem's interest in Christ's descent likely affected the interests of other Christians of his ilk in Edessa, who seem to be the community behind *Doctr. Addai.* On Christ's descent into the underworld in Ephrem's thought, see Teixidor, "Le thème de la descente"; Buchan, *Blessed is He*; and Rouwhorst, "Descent of Christ."

B. *with whom he existed . . . one exalted divinity*: a Nicene statement that also could signal an early miaphysite perspective. In his second letter to Nestorius, Cyril of Alexandria writes: "We do not worship a human being in conjunction with the Logos, lest the appearance of a division creep in by reason of that phrase 'in conjunction with.' No, we worship one and the same, because the body of the Logos is not alien to him but accompanies him even as he is enthroned with the Father" (trans. from Norris, *Christological Controversy*, 134).

C. *How can we receive . . . not ours*: see 93:3–4, where Addai confirms that he has not accepted any gifts or bribes from anyone in the city. Addai's successor Aggai will make a similar claim in 97:3.

D. *Augustina*: Syr. *ʾagūstīn.* This queen mother of Edessa only appears in *Doctr. Addai* and may be entirely fictional. The use of the title "augusta" may be an attempt to liken King Abgar to Constantine, whose mother was traditionally known as Helena Augusta.

E. *Šalmath daughter of Meherdath*: a historical queen of Edessa, though another anachronism. An inscription on a column in the citadel of Edessa from the early third century records: "I Aphtuḥa *nu[hadra?]*, son of Bars[. . .] made this column and the statue which is on it to Shelmath the Queen, daughter of Maʿnu the *pa[ṣ]griba,* wife of the [kin]g my lady [. . .]" (trans. from Ross,

powers which the Lord performed, (and) his divine victories and his ascension to his Father. [2](He recounted) how they received powers and authorities at the time that he was taken up, that very power by which he had healed Abgar and ʿAbdu bar ʿAbdu, the majordomo of his kingdom. [3](He further related) how he had made known to them that he would be revealed at the end of times, at the consummation of all creating beings, at the rising of the dead, which would happen for all people, and at the separation between the sheep and the goats—that is, between believers and infidels.

Acts 1:8–9, 2:1–4

Matt 25:31–46

15 [1](Addai) said to them, "Because the gate of life is narrow and the way of truth is straight, for this reason there are few true believers and Satan's satisfaction comes through infidelity. [2]For this reason, there are many deceivers who lead astray those who see. [3]For if there was not a good end for the faithful, our Lord would not have descended from heaven and come to a birth and a suffering of death. [4]Also, he would not have sent us ourselves[A] so that we might be his preachers and evangelists. [5]But what we saw and heard from him that he did and taught, we proclaim steadfastly before all people so as not to be unjust to the truth of his gospel. [6]Indeed, it is not these matters only, but we proclaim and preach, too, that which happened in his name after his ascension.

Matt 7:14

cf. Matt 7:15

cf. 1 John 1:3

Roman Edessa, 1). The Maʿnu mentioned in the inscription likely refers to the father of Abgar X (r. 239–242 CE), the last king of Edessa. See Drijvers, *Old-Syriac Inscriptions*, no. 27, 19–21; Segal, *Edessa*, 18–19. Meherdath is not found in the inscription, though Tacitus says that a certain King Abgar was involved in a treacherous act against Roman attempts to install a certain Meherdath (Meherdates) as king of Armenia in 49 CE. According to Tacitus, Abgar detained Meherdath and later abandoned him in Adiabene to be defeated by his rival, a pro-Persian candidate to the Armenian throne (*Ann.* 12.12, 14). The veracity of Tacitus's account is uncertain. See Ross, *Roman Edessa*, 10 and a slightly different take by Segal, *Edessa*, 23–24. The two names given in *Doctr. Addai* appear to be historical, though from completely different time periods.

A. *He would not have sent us ourselves*: C has "He would have sent us ourselves." However, the first folio ends here and it may be a corruption. C resumes at ch. 20.

The Finding of the True Cross
by Protonike

16 [1] "Now, I will tell you everything that happened, what was done by people who, like you, believed in Christ, the Son of the Living God. [2]Protonike[A] was the wife of Claudius Caesar, the one whom Tiberius had made second of his kingdom[B] when he

A. *Protonike*: the tale of Protonike finding the True Cross is an expansion on the Helena Augusta legend. The Protonike story situates the *first* finding of the True Cross in the first century. The fact that the Protonike version appears only in Syriac (and later Armenian) sources suggests that this was a local story that probably served some nationalist interests of the Syriac churches. Drijvers and Drijvers (*Finding of the True Cross*, 14–15) link this story and *Doctr. Addai* to Rabbula and give two motives for including it: "1) establishing a relationship between the church of Edessa and Jerusalem; 2) linking the local Eddessene branch of Christianity with the Church of the Empire and the imperial house." These are undoubtedly true, but we also may consider that Syriac Christians were interested in inventing their own versions of popular tales that rivaled or even replaced earlier versions, including martyrdom narratives (e.g., *Mart. Sharb.*), apocryphal acts (e.g., *Hist. John*), and saints' lives (e.g., *Vit. Rab.*, *Vit. Eph.*). The invention of a narrative of finding the true cross fits rightly within this period of development and expansion of the Edessene church. There are good reasons to believe that this story originated independently of *Doctr. Addai*, since it is not found in B (though this version contains several lacunae so we cannot be certain that it was never included). It may have developed around the end of the fourth century and was then incorporated into *Doctr. Addai* by the scribe of the St. Petersburg manuscript (see Drijvers, *Helena Augusta*, 153). The name Protonike ("first victory") is invented and is not a historical wife of Claudius. Drijvers and Drijvers (*Finding of the True Cross*, 15) say the name "has a symbolical meaning and refers to the first victory of the Cross when it was discovered initially." This also clears up the problems of having multiple stories of the finding of the cross in one manuscript.

B. *Claudius Caesar . . . second of his kingdom*: this is the second "Caesar" mentioned by the storyteller (see Tiberius in 1:1). To give the title "Caesar" to Claudius at this point would of course be anachronistic, though it may reflect the storyteller's frame of reference, since he would have known an empire that shared rule between multiple Augusti and Caesari. It is not true that Tiberius made Claudius his second. For one, Claudius succeeded Gaius (Calligula), not Tiberius. For another, Suetonius (*Claud.* 5) says that when Claudius asked to enter the *cursus honorum*, Tiberius granted him consular regalia, but Claudius received no actual responsibilities. After Tiberius ignored Claudius's appeal, the latter resigned himself to a quiet life until he was forced to be emperor following Gaius's assassination in 41 CE. See another mention of Claudius Caesar in ch. 76 below.

went to war against the Spaniards who had rebelled against him.[A] [3]While Shemon,[B] one of the disciples, was in the city of Rome, this woman saw the signs, wonders, and astonishing powers he performed in the name of Christ. [4]She renounced the paganism of her ancestors in which she lived along with the pagan idols which she worshiped. She believed in Christ our Lord so that she worshiped and glorified[C] him together with those who were followers of Shemon and she held him in great honor.[D] [5]After this, she wanted also to see Jerusalem and the places where the mighty deeds of our Lord had been performed. [6]So, zealously, she got up and left Rome for Jerusalem,[E] she and her two sons and her one virgin daughter with her.

A. *went to war . . . against him*: an anachronism. Desreumaux (*Histoire*, 66) suggests that the writer had in mind the situation in Spain during the reign of Marcus Aurelius Claudius (r. 268–270 CE). In a letter to the Senate cited in the *Historia Augusta* 25.7, Claudius says that the territories of Gaul and Spain were under foreign control and the narrator tells that Claudius overcame them. Griffith ("*Doctrina Addai*," 24) argues that, since there was no activity going on in Spain until the early fifth century, the storyteller of *Doctr. Addai* may have in mind Constantius's actions against the Visigoths in 414–416 CE. Ramelli ("Possible Historical Traces," 72–81) suggests that we should take "Spaniards" (lit. "children of Spain"; *bnay 'espny'a*) as a reference to the inhabitants of Hiberia, rather than the Iberians, the former being the group that occupied modern Georgia. Ramelli argues that the reference to Tiberius in conflict with the *Hiberians* is actually historical and points to a conflict with the Parthians in the region of the Hiberians in 35–37 CE. Ramelli summarizes: "The correspondence between Abgar and Jesus should have taken place just in the years 35–36; seen in this light, the reference to the 'children of Spain' (a Semitic periphrasis that stands for 'Hiberi') of Tiberius's letter is not an anachronism, but a precise historical detail" (74).

B. *Shemon*: Simon Peter, whose activities in Rome are recounted in several Syriac texts, including portions of the Pseudo-Clementine *Recognitions*, *Pre. Pet. Rome, Hist. Sim. Ceph.* Peter appears again in Addai's speeches in ch. 93.

C. *glorified*: A has *mšiḥā* but should read *mšabḥā*. See the errata in Phillips, *Doctrine of Addai*, 52.

D. *she held him in great honor*: several traditions note that members of the royal house of Rome converted to Christianity. *Hist. Sim. Ceph.* 29:3, a Syriac tradition, states that many from the house of Caesar converted, noting specifically Agrippa's wives: Agrippina, Crithna, Aphja, and Drosina.

E. *left Rome for Jerusalem*: in the Kyriakos legend (also of Syriac origins), Helena Augusta leads an army to Jerusalem to force the Jews to give up the cross.

17 [1] "When she entered Jerusalem, the city came to meet her and received her with great honor as due the lady empress[A] of the great land of the Romans. [2]Now, James,[B] who was made leader and ruler[C] of the church built there for us, when he heard about why she had come there, he got up and went to her and came before her where she was staying, in the great palace of the royal house of King Herod. [3]When she saw him, she received him with great joy, even as (she had received) Shemon Cephas; and he also showed her healings and miracles like Shemon.

18 [1] "She said to him, 'Show me Golgotha where Christ was crucified, the wood of his cross on which he was hung by the Jews, and the tomb in which he was placed.' [2]James said to her, 'These three things your majesty wishes to see are under the authority of the Jews. [3]They are the ones who hold them and they do not allow us to go pray there before Golgotha and the tomb; nor are they willing to give us the wood of his cross.[D] [4]Not only this, but they also persecute us that we might not preach or proclaim in the name of Christ and many times even imprison us.'[E]

cf. *6 Bks. Dorm.* 2

cf. Acts 5:18; 8:3; 12:4

A. *lady empress*: Syr. *malkthā mārteh*. This title suggests that Claudius in this context is indeed considered a ruler of the Romans, not simply a majordomo. This would confirm that the storyteller sets up Tiberius and Claudius as co-rulers. See the note in 16:2.

B. *James*: lit. "Jacob." That is, James the Just, the head of the church in Jerusalem. See the note about him in Desreumaux, *Histoire*, 125.

C. *leader and ruler*: Syr. *mdabrānā wpāqūdā*. these two terms appear prominently in *Doctr. Addai* (see e.g., chs. 77, 97) as offices of appointment in the church. They are the standard offices in *Teach. Apos.* The use of these terms provides an important continuity between *Doctr. Addai* and *Teach. Apos.*, which appear together in B. They were probably designed to be read together and were edited with such continuity in mind.

D. *do not allow us to pray . . . his cross*: in the various Dormition traditions, including the Syriac *6 Bks. Dorm.*, Jewish leaders seal up the tomb and place guards at the site on orders to kill anyone who goes there to pray. They also hide the cross and other relics.

E. In the Helena Augusta legend, the "persecutors" had placed a shrine dedicated to Venus over the site so that it seemed as though worshipers were visiting the Venus shrine instead of worshiping Christ (see the translation in Drijvers, *Helena Augusta*, 79–80). In the Protonike version, the troublemaking has been transferred onto the Jews, which fits in line with *Doctr. Addai* more generally in its disparagement of Jews.

19 [1] "When she heard these things, immediately the empress ordered they bring before her Onias son of Ḥanan the priest, Gedalia son of Caiaphas, and Judah son of ʿEbed Šalom, the chiefs and rulers of the Jews.[A] [2]She said to them, 'Surrender Golgotha, the tomb, and the wood of the cross to James and his followers. Let no one hinder them from holding services there according to the custom of their worship.'[B] [3]When she had thus ordered the priests, she got up to go and see those places and to hand over that region to James and those who were with him.

Luke 3:2; Acts 4:6

20 [1]"Later, (the empress) entered the tomb and she found within three crosses:[C] one belonging to our Lord, and two belonging to those robbers who were crucified with him, on his right and his left. [2]The moment she went inside the tomb—she and her children with her—her virgin daughter,[D] in that moment, fell down and died, without pain, without sickness, and without cause for death.[E] [3]When the empress saw that her daughter suddenly had died, she knelt down and, praying in the midst of the tomb, she said in her prayer: [4]ʿO God,[F] who gave himself to death for the

Luke 23:33

A. *Onias . . . chiefs and rulers of the Jews*: Ḥanan bar Seth (Annas) was high priest in Jerusalem beginning in 6 CE. Caiaphas took over as priest in 18 CE (Josephus, *A.J.* 20.198 records that five of his sons were a part of the priesthood as well). Both of these men are listed in Acts 4:6 as chief priests. Acts also mentions a Jonathan and an Alexander, but not Judah son of ʿEbed Šalom.

B. Protonike opts to use her imperial power to force the Jews into handing over the site. By contrast, Helena Augusta is led to the correct place by a divine vision.

C. *three crosses*: the discovery of three crosses parallels the finding of the cross by Helena Augusta. The story here is dependent on Luke's gospel account who includes that Jesus was crucified with two others, one on each side of him (Luke 23:33).

D. *virgin daughter*: here begins the second folio of C.

E. In the Helena Augusta legend, no one dies, but an ill woman is found nearby and Helena prays and lays each cross on the ill woman until she is healed by the True Cross. Here, the drama has been intensified by the sudden death of Protonike's virgin daughter and the three distinct prayers for each cross as it is laid on her. In the Kyriakos legend, Judas Kyriakos stops a funeral procession passing by and performs the same test on the dead youth.

F. *God*: in C, "God" (*ʾalāhā*) has been erased by a later hand and replaced with "Son of God" (*brā ʾalāhā*). This change suggests some internal conflicts

sake of all humanity and was crucified in this land and set in this tomb; who rose up and brought to life many with him, just as God gives life to all; to whom neither the crucifying Jews, nor the erring pagans—those whose idols, graven images, and pagan worship I have renounced—will listen.[A] [5]They will look at me with derision and say, "All this that has happened to her is because she renounced the gods whom she worshiped, confessed Christ whom she did not know, and went to honor the region of his tomb and crucifixion."[B] [6]If, my Lord,[C] I am unworthy to be heard on account of my worship of created things[D] instead of you, spare your divine name, lest it be reviled in this land, just as they reviled you at your crucifixion.'

cf. Matt 27:39// Mark 15:9

21 [1]"As she said these words in her prayer and was repeating (it) in the suffering of her outcry[E] to all those who were there, her oldest son approached her and said to her, 'Hear what I say, your majesty: [2]I think in my mind and my reason that my sister's sudden death has not happened in vain. Rather, it was a wonderous occurrence by which God might be glorified, lest his name be reviled, so that those who hear of this might believe. [3]Look: we entered the tomb and found three crosses in it and we do not know which of them is that cross on which Christ was hung. [4]By the death of my sister, we are able to see and learn which is Christ's cross, for Christ will not disregard those who believe in him and seek him.'

22 [1]"Empress Protonike recognized in her mind that her son had spoken these words wisely, justly, and rightly, even though in that moment her soul was very bitter. [2]She took one of the crosses in her hands and placed it on her daughter's corpse which lay

among the groups vying for control over the Addai story and its meaning and significance for Christianity in Edessa in the early fifth century. See the introduction, pp. 14–18.

A. *to whom . . . will listen*: C lacks the negative particle, making it so the Jews and pagans *will* hear/listen.

B. *his tomb and crucifixion*: C has "his tomb and his cross."

C. *My Lord*: lacking in C.

D. *created things*: C has "your created things."

E. *her outcry*: C lacks "her."

before her. ³Then she said in her prayer, 'O God^A who has shown wonderous powers in this land so that we might hear and believe, if this is your cross, my Lord, on which your humanity was hung by insolent people, show the strong and mighty power of your divinity, which dwells in the midst of your humanity, and let this daughter of mine live and rise up so that your name may be glorified when her soul returns to her body. ⁴May those who crucified you be ashamed but may those who worship you rejoice.' After she said this, she waited a long moment.

23 ¹"Then she took up that cross from her daughter's corpse and placed another (on her). ²Again, she said in her prayer: 'O God,^B by whose beckoning the worlds and creatures exist, who takes pleasure in the lives of all people who turn toward him, and who does not turn away from those who beseech him, if this is your cross, my Lord, show the power of your triumphs just as you customarily do, and let this daughter of mine live and rise. ³May the pagans who worship your creatures,^C rather than you, be ashamed and may the true believers confess so that their mouth might be opened to glorify you before those who reject you.' ⁴She waited a long moment after (saying) these things and she took up the second cross from her daughter.^D

24 ¹"Then she took up the third cross and placed it on her daughter. ²And just as she was about to lift her eyes to heaven and open her mouth in prayer, immediately, in that moment, like an eyelid flaps over the eye,^E as the cross touched her daughter's

A. *O God*: C has "O Christ."

B. *O God*: once again, C replaces "God" with "Son of God" (see above in ch. 20). This edit appears to be by the same hand as the earlier one.

C. *your creatures*: C just has "creatures."

D. *She waited . . . from her daughter*: C contains an additional word here (*rūḥā*=spirit), so that the sentence reads: "The Spirit waited a long time after these things."

E. *like an eyelid flaps over the eye*: parallel to the English idiom "in the blink of an eye."

corpse, her daughter came to life and at once[A] stood up and glorified[B] God who had given her life by means of his cross.

25 [1]"Then, seeing how her daughter was brought to life, Empress Protonike was troubled and very frightened. [2]But though she was frightened, she glorified Christ and believed in him, that he is the Son of the living God. [3]Her son said to her, 'You have seen, my lady, that if this had not happened today, perhaps they may have left this cross of Christ, by which my sister came to life, and they may have taken and honored one belonging to those murderous robbers. [4]Now, look: we have seen and rejoiced that Christ has been glorified by this (miracle) he has performed.'

cf. Matt 16:16

26 [1]"Then (Protonike) took up Christ's cross and gave it to James so that it might be kept in great honor. [2]She then ordered that a great and excellent building be constructed on Golgotha where (Christ) was crucified as well as over the tomb where he was laid so that these places might be honored and that there might be an appointed place there for prayer and an assembly for worship.[C]

27 [1]"Then, when the empress saw all the citizens who had gathered for this spectacle of this occurrence, she ordered that her daughter should go with her openly, without the suitable royal veil, to the palace of the king where she was staying, in order that everyone might see her and glorify God.[D]

28 [1]"Now the crowd of Jews and pagans, who had rejoiced and were glad at the beginning of this affair, were very sad at its culmination. [2]For they would have been pleased if this affair they had seen had not happened, for because of it many had believed in Christ. [3]Now, increasingly, they saw that many of the signs that

A. *at once*: lacking in C.

B. *glorified*: the second folio of C ends here.

C. Helena Augusta is not said to have set up a place of worship in the earliest version of the story (from Rufinus). However, she does tear down the shrine to Venus and rids the place where the cross laid of all semblance of paganism. In contrast to this, the Protonike legend creates an origin story here for the Church of the Holy Sepulchre. Egeria visited this site while she was in Jerusalem, so a shrine must have existed in the 380s.

D. Similarly, in the Kyriakos legend, people witness the resurrection of the dead youth and they are amazed.

happened in his name after the ascension[A] were greater in number than those that happened before his ascension.

29 [1]"Moreover, news of this event that had transpired traveled to remote places, even to my fellow apostles who were preaching Christ. [2]So there was peace in the churches of Jerusalem and its surrounding cities and those who had not seen this occurrence glorified God along with those who had seen it.

30 [1]"As the empress went up from Jerusalem to the city of Rome, every city she entered crowded together to catch a glimpse of her daughter. [2]When she entered Rome, she recounted what had happened before Claudius Caesar. [3]When Caesar heard (the story), he ordered all the Jews to vacate the land of Italy, since the occurrence was being talked about by many people throughout the whole region.[B] [4](Protonike), moreover, told Shemon Cephas what had happened.

Acts 18:2

The Apostles and Their Acts

31 [1]"Therefore, everything our fellow apostles were doing we proclaim to everyone so that those who do not know might also hear what Christ was doing through us openly, so that our Lord may be glorified by all people. [2]I have narrated these (stories) before you so that you may know and understand how great the faith of Christ is for those who truly believe.

A. *the ascension*: the pronominal suffix *-h* has a dot over it, indicating the feminine third-singular suffix: "her ascension." Howard (*Teaching of Addai*, 109) took this as a scribal error and translated it as masculine (see also Phillips, *Doctrine of Addai*, 15). Desreumaux (*Histoire*, 72) has "aprés son ascension," while Illert (*Doctrina Addai*, 145) has "vor seiner Himmelfahrt." I have chosen not to represent the pronoun in question at all.

B. In the Kyriakos legend, Helena also stirs up a persecution of the Jews because of their impediment in the finding of the True Cross. This version clearly intends to align itself with the Protonike story, as Drijvers surmises. Its focus on the Jews as the primary antagonists creates an obvious link between the two narratives. The mention of Claudius in the context of expelling the Jews from Rome also brings *Doctr. Addai* in line with Acts 18:2 which mentions the edict of Claudius expelling the Jews, and which Suetonius records famously as instigated by "Chrestus," a possible mistake for "Christos." See Suetonius, *Claud.* 5.25.

32 ¹"Then James, the leader of the Jerusalem church, who had seen the event with his own eyes, wrote about it and sent it to my fellow apostles in the cities of their regions. ²Those apostles also wrote accounts and informed James of everything Christ had done through them. ³These accounts were read before the whole congregation of the people of the church."[A]

The Marshaling of Edessa

33 ¹When King Abgar heard these things, he, Augustina[B] his mother, Šalmath daughter of Meherdath, Paqūr,[C] ʿEbedšamaš, Šamašgram, ʿAbdu, Azzai,[D] and Bar Kalbā,[E] along with the rest of

A. *These accounts were read . . . church*: in Acts 15:4 Paul and Barnabas report their work among the gentiles to the "church and the apostles and the elders" in Jerusalem. It does not indicate that these were written accounts. The storyteller of *Doctr. Addai* probably has in mind various acts, some of which had been composed and/or translated into Syriac at this point. See Desreumaux, *Histoire*, 73–74 n. 69.

B. *Augustina*: the fictional mother of Abgar here is almost certainly meant to create a connection between Abgar–Augustina and Constantine–Helena Augusta, who later (re)discovered the True Cross.

C. *Paqūr*: this person is only mentioned here. The name is obscure and may be semantically related to the verb *pqr*, which refers to being insane with anger.

D. *Azzai*: this person is only mentioned here. The meaning of the name may be connected to a second- or third-century mosaic from Edessa which contains a family portrait (see Drijvers, *Old-Syriac Inscriptions*, no. 47 l. 6). The name in the mosaic has been damaged but begins with ʾz... and may contain a *yod* after the *zayn* (see Segal, *Edessa*, pl. I). If this mosaic does contain a portrait and reference to Azzai, it would make sense that the storyteller would attempt to connect an early noble family, whose portrait still survived in the city, to the narrative of Christian expansion into Edessa.

E. *Bar Kalbā*: lit. "son of a dog." This person features throughout the text (see chs. 35, 66, 78). He is also mentioned in *Mart. Sharb.* and *Mart. Bars.* (cf. ch. 68). This name is found in several old Syriac inscriptions discovered in a cave approximately 100 km southeast of Edessa, as well as in a deed of sale written in Syriac from Dura-Europos, dated 243 CE. See Drijvers, *Old Syriac Inscriptions*, nos. 6–8. On the deed of sale see Torrey, "Syriac Parchment from Edessa." The name Bar Kalbā is mentioned in these inscriptions as the father of Ḥaphsai, a name that appears in several traditions, including *Mart. Sharb.* and *Mart. Ait.*

their companions, rejoiced greatly and they all glorified God and confessed Christ.

[2]King Abgar said to Addai, "I wish for you to speak openly before the entire city everything that we have heard from you today as well as the rest of the other matters so that everyone may hear the preaching of the gospel of Christ, which you are teaching us; [3]that they might be contented and established in the instruction which you are teaching us; that many might understand that justly I have believed in Christ, through the letter I sent to him; [4]that they might understand that the Son of God is God, that you are his true and faithful disciple; [5]and that you show his glorious power by actions in front of those who are willing to believe in him."

34 [1]The next day, Abgar ordered 'Abdu bar 'Abdu—the one who had been healed from his severe disease of his feet—to send a herald to call the entire city that all citizens should assemble, men and women, to the placed called Beth Tbārā,[A] a large region belonging to the house of 'Awidā son of 'Ebednahad,[B] so that they might hear the teaching of Addai the apostle: how he taught, in whose name he healed, by what power he performed signs and did wonders. [2]For when he had healed king Abgar, only the nobles had been present before him and had seen him as he healed the one whom many physicians were unable to heal, by the word of Christ. [3]A foreigner healed him by the faith of Christ.

A. *Beth Tbārā*: lit. "House of Fracture." *Chron. Ed.* mentions that Abgar had a winter palace at Beth Tbārā that was destroyed in the flood of 202 CE. See Guidi, *Chronica Minora I*, 4.

B. *'Awidā son of 'Ebednahad*: a variation of the name 'Ebednahad is found in a sketch of a second- or third-century mosaic, the so-called mosaic of Zendora (now lost) (Drijvers, *Old Syriac Inscriptions*, no. 44). This person is mentioned throughout *Doctr. Addai*, usually in conjunction with Bar Kalbā (see chs. 35 and 66). Significantly, 'Awidā is also the name of a follower of Bardaisan, in this case the addressee of *Bk. Laws*. In *Doctr. Addai*, 'Awidā is portrayed as a convert to the Christianity of Addai, which we may recognize as part of the polemic of pro-Nicene Christians against Bardaisanite Christians. Other polemics are also evident in the names included in *Doctr. Addai*. We have seen repeated occurrence of Šmešgrām, who also is named as a friend of Bardaisan in *Bk. Laws*. 'Awidā is also mentioned in *Mart. Sharb.* and *Mart. Bars.*

35 [1]When the entire city had assembled, men and women, just as the king had ordered, 'Awidā, Lebbu,[A] Ḥaphsai,[B] Bar Kalbā, Lebubnā,[C] Ḥasrun,[D] and Šmešgrām were standing there along with their companions who, like them, were the king's chiefs and nobles. [2]All the officers, workers, handcrafters, both Jews and pagans who were in the city, foreigners of the countries of Ṣobā[E] and Ḥārrān[F] and the rest of the inhabitants of the region of Mesopotamia[G]—all of them were present to hear the teaching of Addai, about whom they had heard he was a disciple of Jesus, who had been crucified in Jerusalem, and that he was performing healings in his name.

A. *Lebbu*: this person is only mentioned here. The name comes from the root *lb* for "heart." The same name appears also in *Mart. Sharbel*.

B. *Ḥaphsai*: this name figures prominently in a number of stories from Edessa and from Adiabene. The name is mentioned among the nobility who convert in *Mart. Sharb.*, which appears in B alongside *Doctr. Addai*, and the Sharbel narrative is literarily related to *Mart. Ait.*, where Ḥaphsai is said to be a Christian priest. The name also appears in *Mart. Bars.*, which also shares a literary relationship with *Mart. Sharb.* All this is to say that the frequency of occurrence of these names suggests, as Brock ("Eusebius," 228) argues, that all of these narratives originated in the same circles in Edessa. We may also suggest that, given their proximity in the manuscripts, the texts were edited by particular scribes to include the same names of certain noble houses.

C. *Lebubnā*: the same name that occurs in ch. 103 for the famous scribe of Edessa who evidently placed *Doctr. Addai* in the civic archives. See the note in ch. 103.

D. *Ḥasrun*: this name is only mentioned here. The verb *ḥsar* means to be lacking or wanting in something.

E. *Ṣobā*: one of the Syriac names for the city of Nisibis. The latter name may be traced back to the Assyrian name *Naṣibīna* and the former comes from the city's identification with the biblical town of *Ṣōbā* (cf. 2 Sam. 8:1). See Takahashi, "Nisibis."

F. *Ḥārrān*: Lat. *Carrhae*, about 45 km southeast of Edessa. The Arab geographer Yāqūt records the tradition that this was the first city built after the Flood and was visited by Abraham. Ḥārrān was a center for the cult of Sin, a moon god, but throughout late antiquity the town was Christian and even was home to a few Syrian Orthodox Patriarchs for a few brief periods. See Takahashi, "Ḥārrān"; Possekel, "Transformation of Harran."

G. *the region of Mesopotamia*: this parallels the statement in *Teach. Apos.* 6:9 that Addai evangelized the "border regions of Mesopotamia" (trans. Witakowski, *MNTA*).

The Teaching of Addai

36 [1]Addai began to speak to them as follows:[A]
[2]"Listen, all of you, and understand what I am about to tell you. I am not a physician with drugs and herbs of human craft.[B] [3]Rather, I am a disciple of Jesus Christ, the physician of troubled souls, the savior of the future life, the Son of God who descended from heaven, put on the body[C] and became a human being, gave himself, and was crucified on behalf of all humanity. [4]When he was hung on the tree, the sun in the firmament went dark.[D] [5]After he entered the tomb, he was raised and left the tomb with many others. [6]Those who were keeping watch over the tomb did not see how he went forth from the tomb.[E] [7]The Watchers[F] on high became heralds and preachers of his resurrection.

Mark 15:33 par.

Matt 27:52

cf. Luke 24:4–7

A. This portion of Addai's instruction continues to ch. 61. As Camplani ("Traditions," 269) writes, there are three major speeches in *Doctr. Addai* that consist of material distinct from the Eusebian legend. Camplani argues that in these speeches we come to see a clear relationship inferred between Christianity and the state.

B. *I am not a physician with drugs and herbs of human craft*: this statement harkens back to Abgar's letter. Addai is thus a true representative of Jesus, since he heals in the same manner. The ability to heal without drugs is a common feature of Christian heroes in Syriac myths. In *Mart. Nars.* (trans. in Herman, *Persian Martyr Acts*, 2) a similar claim is made about Christians in general—that they do not use medicines to heal but heal by divine power.

C. *put on the body*: a typical symbol for the incarnation in early Syriac tradition. It is used throughout *Doctr. Addai* and serves as the primary incarnational motif for Addai throughout his speech. Fourth-century Syriac sources especially use this symbol. See Brock, *Luminous Eye*, 39; Murray, *Symbols*, 69–94.

D. *the sun in the firmament went dark*: as Desreumaux points out (*Histoire*, 76–77 n. 77), the darkening of the sun is a leit-motif that is repeated several times in Addai's teaching (cf. chs. 42, 55, and 74). The interest in the sun darkening may be a critique levied against the Manichaean "prayer in the sun," which is also critiqued by Augustine (*Haer.* 46.18).

E. *did not see how he went forth from the tomb*: *Gos. Pet.* 35–44 explains how Jesus came forth from the tomb and was seen by the guards exiting with two others. No Syriac translation of *Gos. Pet.* survives so it is not clear if the storyteller of *Doctr. Addai* would have known this tradition.

F. *Watchers*: (or "Wakers") refers to the angelic beings from *1 Enoch* (see also Dan 4:13 and *Jub.* 5). The Watchers have a distinct status within early Syriac ascetic discourse as models for the *qaddišin* ("holy ones") (see Brock, *Luminous Eye*, 140–41). Here the allusion to the Watchers/Wakers may be

37 [1]"He would not have died, if he had not wished to, since he is Lord of the boundary of death. [2]If it had not pleased him, he would not have put on the body again—indeed, it was through him that the body was fashioned. [3]For that desire which inclined him to be born of the Virgin also humbled him to the suffering of death. [4]He who had been with his Father from the beginning and from eternity humbled the greatness of his exalted divinity.[A]

38 [1]"He of whom the prophets of a former time spoke in their mysteries and described the symbols[B] of his birth, his suffering, his resurrection, his ascension to his Father, and his seat at the right hand (of the Father).[C] [2]Look: he is worshiped by heavenly (beings) and mortals—he who was worshiped from eternity.

39 [1]"For although his appearance was of human beings, his power, knowledge, and authority was of God, just as he said to us: [2]'Look: from now on the Son of Man is glorified and God, who is in him, glorifies him with powers, wonders, and his own honor, which is from his right hand.'[D] [3]His body is the pure purple

cf. Phil 2:7

cf. John 17:1–5

---

closer to the Parable of the Virgins in Matt 25, since in this context the "waking" of the dead comes from Matt 27, to which Addai alludes in the previous line.

A. *He would not have died . . . his exalted divinity*: this paragraph may be compared with Cyril of Alexandria's second letter to Nestorius (*Ep.* 4; trans. from Norris, *Christological Controversy*, 134): "And for the Logos to become flesh is nothing other than for him to 'share in flesh and blood as we do' [Heb. 2:14], to make his own a body from among us, and to be born of a woman as a human being. He did not depart from his divine status or cease to be born of the Father; he continued to be what he was, even in taking on flesh."

B. *symbols*: Syr. *demwāthā* can be used to render the Greek τύποι. Syriac writers such as Ephrem were fond of the use of "symbols" or "types" in their theological expression. See Murray, *Symbols*; and den Biesen, *Simple and Bold*.

C. *symbols of his birth . . . right hand (of the Father)*: the sequence of these sentences follows that of both the Apostolic Creed and the Nicene Creed.

D. *Look! . . . from his right hand*: the saying is not a direct quotation of John 17:1–5 but the content is similar. It is possible that this matches a reading from the *Diatessaron* more closely. The portion of Ephrem's commentary on the *Diatessaron* that refers to John 17:1–5 comments on Christ's presence and activity in the act of creating, which certainly highlights the "power, knowledge, and authority of God" of which Addai speaks here. Cf. McCarthy, *Saint Ephrem's Commentary*, 290–91. The use of the *Diatessaron* would make sense,

garment of his glorious divinity, by which we are able to see his hidden lordship.[A]

40 [1]"Therefore, we preach and proclaim this Jesus Christ, we glorify his Father with him, and we exalt and worship the Spirit of his divinity, for thus we were commanded by him, that we baptize and make atonement for those who believe in the name of the Father and the Son and the Spirit of Holiness. Even the prophets of a former time said that the Lord our God would send us his Spirit.

cf. Matt 28:19
Isa 48:16

41 [1]"But if I am saying something not written in the Prophets, then the Jews who stand among you and listen to me will not receive it. [2]And if, moreover, I make mention of Christ's name over those who have diseases and maladies and they are not cured by this glorious name, then those who worship the makings of their hands will not believe. [3]But if those things of which we speak are written in the books[B] and the Prophets, and we are able to demonstrate healing powers upon the sick, then no one will say of us that it is by faith[C] without discernment that we preach that God was crucified on behalf of all humanity.[D]

---

since it is said to be the version of the Gospel read in churches in ch. 71.

A. *His body . . . his hidden lordship*: to Nestorius, Cyril of Alexandria writes: "we say that in an unspeakable and incomprehensible way, the Logos united to himself, in his hypostasis, flesh enlivened by a rational soul, and in this way became a human being and has been designated 'Son of man.' He did not become a human being simply by an act of will or 'good pleasure,' any more than he did so by merely taking on a person" (*Ep.* 4; trans. from Norris, *Christological Controversy*, 133).

B. *the books*: Syr. *sepre*. This term usually refers to books of the Bible. In this case, it probably is in reference to the Torah, i.e., the first five books of the Jewish Bible. The appeal to prophecy and what is found in Scripture is a common motif in Jewish/Christian polemics.

C. Here begins the text of B. The first folio is faded and damaged, so some words are difficult to decipher.

D. *God was crucified . . . humanity*: Griffith suggests, "It would be hard not to recognize in the phrase 'God was crucified for all people,' a representation of the Christology of those whom their adversaries, after the time of the council of Chalcedon (451) would label 'Monophysites.' To put it forward as the historical faith of Edessa suggests that the author of the *Doctrina Addai* was interested in propounding the christological view associated with Cyril of Alexandria (d. 444) in the context of the controversies of his own day" ("Doctrina Addai," 288–89).

42 [1]"And if there are those who are not willing to be persuaded by these words, let them approach us and make known their opinion, so that, like a malady of their mind, we might offer a healing remedy for the convalescence of their disease. [2]For though you were not present at the moment of Christ's suffering, nevertheless, by the sun which you saw become dark,[A] learn and understand about the great and terrible event that happened at the moment of the crucifixion of him whose gospel has spread throughout the whole world through the wonders which our fellow disciples are doing throughout the whole world.

Mark 15:33 par.

43 [1]"Those who were Hebrews and who knew only the Hebrew language with which they were born, look: today they speak in all languages so that those who were far away may hear and believe just as those who were near, that he was the one who confounded the languages of those insolent people who inhabited this region before us.[B] [2]He is the one who teaches today the just and true faith through us imperfect, wretched people from Galilee of Palestine.

Acts 2:6–12

cf. Eph 2:17

Gen 11:6–9

44 [1]"For even I whom you see am from Paneas,[C] the place from which the Jordan River flows forth. [2]I was chosen with my companions to be a preacher[D] of this gospel, through which, look:

A. *by the sun which you saw become dark*: implies that, although the doubters "were not present" at the crucifixion, they would have seen the darkening of the sun from anywhere. In his commentary on the *Diatessaron* (21.4), Ephrem the Syrian says the sun darkened as a result of Nature itself reacting to Christ's death.

B. *the one who confounded . . . this region before us*: an allusion to the story of Babel in Gen 11. The story of Babel is set in Mesopotamia and thus the Christian natives of Edessa may have seen themselves as ethnically descended from such cultures. The continued use of the Seleucid calendar by Syriac writers throughout late antiquity shows that these groups continued pre-Christian notions of identity and culture for some time after Christianization.

C. *Paneas*: Banias in Syria, known in the New Testament as Caesarea-Philippi. The Nahal Hermon (also known as the Banias River) is, in fact, one of the tributaries of the Jordan River. Eusebius (*Hist. eccl.* 7.17–18) mentions Paneas as the hometown of the bleeding woman from Matt 9:20–26. The name of the city is related to the Greek god Pan and Eusebius describes a festival to the god that involved casting a sacrificial victim into the river. See also Desreumaux, *Histoire*, 128.

D. Here begins a lacuna in B (fol. 1r). The bottom portion of the manuscript has been lost. Since this is the first surviving page of the manuscript it

districts in every place are resounding with the glorious name of the august Christ.

45 [1]"Therefore, let none of you be close-minded[A] to what is just or forsake[B] the truth. [2]Do not be captivated by thoughts of destructive error which are full of the despair of bitter death.[C] [3]Do not be taken by evil customs of the paganism of your ancestors so that you abstain from a life of justice and truth that is in Christ. [4]For those who believe in him are those who are entrusted before him who descended to us by his[D] grace so that he might remove pagan sacrifices from the world, along with the idolatrous libations, so that created things might no longer be worshiped. [5]Rather, let us worship him and his Father with his Spirit of Holiness.

46 [1]"For my part,[E] just as my Lord commanded me, look: I preach and proclaim the gospel. [2]Look: I place his silver upon the table before you and I sow the seed of his word in the ears of all humankind.[F] [3]Those who wish to receive it will have a good

cf. Matt 25:14–25// Luke 19:12–23

cf. Mark 4:1–9 par.

---

is not surprising that it has succumbed to some damage. In the first few folios there are several lacunae.

A. *close-minded*: lit. "be hard in his mind." Such a state of being would be contrary to King Abgar's mindset, which is one of faith. The theme of faith among those not present in Jerusalem to witness Christ's miracles and teachings is a major theme in *Doctr. Addai*.

B. *forsake*: lit. "to remove his mind." In Syriac this is a bit of play on words, encouraging the hearers not to be closeminded, nor to empty their minds completely.

C. *the despair of bitter death*: the Syriac is unclear. This may be a reference to sacrificial cultic practices, which are viewed negatively throughout the narrative. The word *psāq* in its basic sense has to do with cutting or mutilation. The combination with the phrase *dmawtā mrīrā* ("of bitter death") may bring to mind the mutilation of a sacrifice. The next sentence makes this a plausible interpretation, since Addai mentions the "pagan" practices of the ancestors of Edessa. Through the course of his speech, Addai discusses the uselessness of sacrifices and God's plan to abolish them completely through Christ.

D. *his*: A has the feminine pronominal suffix.

E. B resumes here (fol. 1v).

F. *Look: I place . . . all humankind*: allusions to the parables of the Talents and of the Sower. In Ephrem's commentary on the *Diatessaron*, these two parables appear in this same order. See McCarthy, *Saint Ephrem's*

germination of faith. [4]But those who are not persuaded, I will shake off the dust of my feet at them, just as my Lord[A] told me. [5]Repent, therefore, my beloved, from wicked ways and from hateful deeds and turn to him with a good and pleasing will, just as he has turned to you with his grace and his rich mercies.[B] [6]Do not be like former generations that have passed away: because they were close-minded against the fear of God, they received punishment publicly so that they might be chastened and that those who come after them might tremble and fear.

Mark 6:11 par.

cf. Acts 7:51–52

47 [1]"For all of that for which the Lord came to the world was to teach us and to show us that at the end of creation[C] there will be a resurrection for all people. [2]At that time, their customs will be represented in their persons and their bodies will be parchments for the records of justice.[D] [3]There will not be anyone there who cannot read, for every person will read the writings of their own book[E] on that day and will hold an account of their actions on the fingers of their hands. [4]Moreover, the ignorant will learn a new writing of a new language and no one will say to their friend, "Read this to me," for one teaching and one instruction will rule over all people.[F]

Commentary, 184.

A. *my Lord*: lacking in B.

B. *with his grace and in his rich mercies*: B has "with the grace of his mercies."

C. *creation*: A has plural "creatures." I have followed B and Desreumaux in translating it as singular. Howard, *Teaching of Addai*, 47 has "created things."

D. *their bodies will be parchments for the records of justice*: the concept of a book of records of one's deeds is an old one. See Isa 65:6; Ps 56/55:9; Dan 7:10; *1 En* 81:1–2; *Ascen. Isa.* 9.22–23. The same motif appears in *Hist. John* 22. *Doctr. Addai*, for its part, adds the unique dimension that each person's "book" is their own body and their deeds will be written there. See the comments by Desreaumaux, *Histoire*, 130.

E. Here begins a lacuna in B; the text resumes in ch. 54.

F. *no one will say . . . over all people*: this recalls Neh 8:1–8 and Ezra's reading and interpretation of the Law at the constitution of the second Temple. In the sense here, no one would need interpretation if the "correct" instruction (i.e., Addai's instruction as the storyteller presents it) is maintained. It is thus a reversal of Nehemiah.

48 [1]"Therefore, let this thought be depicted before your eyes and let it not escape your mind. [2]For if it should escape your mind, it shall not escape justice. [3]But seek God's mercy so that he might forgive the hateful infidelity of your paganism. [4]You have forsaken the one who created you on the face of the earth and causes his rain to fall and his sun to shine on you, and in his place, you have worshiped his creations.

cf. Rom 11:30–31

cf. Matt 5:45

cf. Rom 1:20

49 [1]"For the idols and graven images of paganism and everything in creation upon which you rely and you worship, if there is any sense or discernment in them, for which reason you worship them and honor them, then it is right that they should offer you a blessing, since you carved and constructed them and you strengthened and fastened them with nails, so that they cannot be shaken. [2]For if created things were to perceive your adulation towards them, they would cry out to you, calling to you: 'Do not worship your fellows who, like you, were made and created,' for creatures were not made to be worshiped. [3]Rather, they should worship their creator and praise the one who created them. [4]Inasmuch as his grace protects the headstrong here, so will his justice be required of the infidels there.[A]

50 [1]"For I see that this city is packed with paganism that is against God. [2]Who is this Nebo, the fabricated idol which you worship, and Bel whom you honor?[B] [3]Look: there are some among you who worship Bāt Nikal,[C] like your neighbors the inhabitants of

---

A. *For the idols . . . the infidels there*: this paragraph begins the invective against the paganism of Edessa. The arguments here and throughout this section are reminiscent of Wis 15, which itself inspired the admonishing of Paul in Romans 1. On Wis in Syriac, see Skelton and Lollar, "Wisdom of Solomon." According to Drijvers (*Cults and Beliefs*, 40–42), "The information yielded by the *Doctrina Addai* regarding pagan cults at other places . . . turns out to be very precise, both in regard to the deities as well as to the sites at which they were worshipped."

B. *Nebo . . . and Bel*: two Babylonian deities who serve as the primary gods being worshiped in pagan Edessa, according to *Doctr. Addai*. This is testified also by *Mart. Sharb.* and by Jacob of Serugh's *Homily on the Fall of the Idols*. On Nebo and Bel in Edessa see Drijvers, *Cults and Beliefs*, 40–75. On Jacob's homily see Schwartz, "Discourses of Religious Violence."

C. *Bāt Nikal*: lit. "Daughter of Nikal" = Ishtar, equated in the Roman pantheon with Venus. The cult of Ishtar is well-attested in Ḥarrān. She was the

Ḥārrān; and Tarʿatha,[A] like the inhabitants of Mabbug;[B] and the eagle,[C] like the Arabs; and the sun and moon,[D] like the rest of the inhabitants of Ḥārrān who are like you.[E]

51 [1]"Do not be captivated by rays of light or the radiant star,[F] for whosoever worships created things is cursed before God. [2]For although there are among created things those which are greater than their fellow creatures, nevertheless their natures[G]

Deut 27:15; Wis 14:8

---

consort and partner of Sin the moon god, both of whom were prominent deities in the city.

A. *Tarʿatha*: also known as Atargatis, the "Syrian Goddess," whose most famous cultic center was Hierapolis/Mabbug. Atargatis was often conflated in inscriptions and iconography with the Greek goddess Artemis. In *Hist. John*, Artemis and her cult are the primary enemies of the apostle John. On this goddess and her cult in Edessa see Drijvers, *Cults and Beliefs*; and Lightfoot, *Lucian*.

B. *Mabbug*: also known as Hierapolis, about 100 km southwest of Edessa. This was a major metropolitan city and was home to several major cults. See Drijvers, *Cults and Beliefs*.

C. *the eagle*: Syr. *nešrā*. Burkitt ("Appendix") hypothesized that this is a textual error and that the text should read *dešrā* = Dusares, the chief deity of the Nabatean Arabs. Drijvers (*Cults and Beliefs*, 41) demonstrates against Burkitt that there is strong evidence for the cult of the eagle in the vicinity of Hatra, so the text need not be amended at all.

D. *sun and moon*: a late second-century inscription in Edessa is dedicated to the moon god Sin, whose cultic center was in nearby Ḥārrān (see Segal, *Edessa*, 57; Drijvers, *Old-Syriac Inscriptions*, no. 14). Emperor Julian wrote about sun worship in Edessa in his Hymn to King Helios (*Oration 4*), given in December 362: "The inhabitants of Edessa, a place from time immemorial sacred to Helios, associate him with Monimos and Azizos" (trans. from Drijvers, *Cults and Beliefs*, 147; see also pp. 122–45 on Sin and pp. 146–74 on Helios).

E. *who are like you*: the meaning is not clear. Probably it intends to suggest that the Edessenes are like the rest of the peoples listed, not just the inhabitants of Ḥārrān. Desreumaux suggests a possible correction of "the Sun and the Moon like the rest of the others who are like you."

F. *radiant star*: probably Venus, which goes by different names, including al-ʿUzza, balti, and, in Syriac, *kawkabthā*. Ephrem also mentions the cult of Venus in *Haer.* 8.10–14; 9.8; 41.4. See Drijvers, *Cults and Beliefs*, 42 n. 9 for other references.

G. *natures*: the concept of nature here (Syr. *knūthe*) is a philosophical concept in these sections of *Doctr. Addai* designating the existential differences between God and human beings, and between Creator and creatures. Significantly, it is this type of philosophical precision that was so important

are those of their fellow (creatures), as I have told you. [3]This is a bitter disease, for which there is no cure, namely that fabrications should worship fabrications and the creatures should praise fellow (creatures). [4]For just as they are unable to stand by their own ability, but only by the ability of the one who created them, so it follows that they not be worshiped alongside (the creator) or be honored alongside the Creator. [5]It is blasphemy against both of them—against the creature, since it is being worshipped, and against the creator, since creatures who are foreign to the nature of the Creator's being are associated with the Creator.[A]

52 [1]"The whole of the prophecy from the prophets and of our own preaching after the prophets is this: creatures should not be worshiped alongside the Creator. [2]Again: human beings should not be bound to the yoke of destructive paganism.[B] [3]Now, it is not (only) on account of creatures which are seen that I am saying they should not be worshiped, but everything that is fabricated, whether seen or unseen, is a creature. [4]This is bitter impiety, that a person should afford it the glorious title of divinity. [5]For it is not creatures that we proclaim or, like you, worship, but the Lord of creatures. [6]The earthquake that shook them by means of the cross is testimony that everything which is fabricated hinges on and lives by[C] the power of the Maker—the one who existed before the

to the christological controversies stirring in the fifth century. *Doctr. Addai* thus appears to be involved in this discussion to a degree.

A. *since creatures who are foreign . . . with the Creator*: this discussion of nature and wrongly directed worship is reminiscent of Wis 13, though such tropes against idolatry are quite common in early Christian literature. As Desreumaux points out, such arguments became a central concern of Islam: falsely associating the nature of the created with that of the Creator.

B. *destructive paganism*: this section may reveal a possible *raison d'être* for *Doctr. Addai*: to combat local adherence to paganism. In A, *Doctr. Addai* appears alongside texts like *Pre. Pet. Rom.* and *Hist. John*, both of which are concerned with the apostolic battle against paganism. In B, likewise, *Doctr. Addai* appears with texts like *Mart. Sharb.*, which has as its main plot line the conversion and eventual martyrdom of a pagan priest of Bel and Nebo. While there are multiple polemics at work in *Doctr. Addai*, the one against paganism is quite prominent and interplays with other texts in the manuscripts as well.

C. *hinges on and lives by*: this appears to be a play on words in the context of the gospel narrative. The earthquake at the cross refers to Matt 27:51. The two verbs that follow both evoke Christ's crucifixion and resurrection: *tlā*

Wis 13:16

worlds and creatures; the one whose nature is incomprehensible, because his nature is invisible; the one who is sanctified with his Father in the highest heights, because he is both Lord and God from eternity.[A]

53 [1]"This is our teaching in every country and in every region and thus we were ordered to preach to those who will listen to us, not with force,[B] but with the teaching of truth and by the power of God. [2]The signs that happened in his name testify about our faith, that it is true and faithful. [3]Therefore, be persuaded by my words and receive everything that I have said and continue to say to you. [4]And so that I do not require your death, look: I increase my admonition before you. Receive my words rightly and do not delay! [5]Draw near to me, you who are far off from Christ, that you may be ones who are near to Christ. [6]Instead of erroneous sacrifices and libations, offer to him sacrifices of thanksgiving from now on.

cf. Mark 9:38//Luke 9:49; Mark 16:20; Acts 2:43; 2 Cor 12:12

cf. Eph 2:13, 17

---

refers to hanging on something, as Jesus hung on the cross, and metaphorically refers to depending on something; and *qāem* comes from the root *qām*, the term typically used to describe the resurrection in Syriac literature. Just as Christ was hung on the cross, so everything hinges on this event, and just as Christ lives and is no longer dead, so all things exist. This is a brilliant use of symbolic language that is admittedly difficult to render into English.

A. *the one who existed before . . . God from eternity*: reminiscent of Cyril of Alexandria's second letter to Nestorius: "we say that in an unspeakable and incomprehensible way, the Logos united to himself, in his hypostasis, flesh enlivened by a rational soul, and in this way became a human being and has been designated 'Son of Man.' . . . This is the sense in which we confess one Christ and Lord. We do not worship a human being in conjunction with the Logos, lest the appearance of a division creep in by reason of that phrase 'in conjunction with.' No, we worship one and the same, because the body of the Logos is not alien to him but accompanies him even as he is enthroned with the Father" (trans. from Norris, *Christological Controversy*, 133–34).

B. *not with force*: the storyteller periodically emphasizes that no one was forced to convert to Addai's gospel. See similar statements in chs. 67 and 80. Camplani ("Traditions," 270) proposes that the exhortation to conversion without force or compulsion constructs an ideal scenario of conversion and may be a (veiled?) critique of Constantinopolitan policies and laws. As Camplani points out, there are interesting parallels here with the representation of conversion tactics in the *Vita Constantini* and the *Actus Silvestri*.

Attacks on Paganism

54 [1]"Now, what is the great altar that was built for you in the middle of this city, where you come and go pouring out libations on it to demons and sacrificing on it to devils?[A] [2]Even if you do not know the Scriptures, has nature not taught you by its insight that your idols have eyes that do not see? [3]You who see with eyes[B] with which you do not perceive; you have become like those who cannot see and cannot hear. [4]It is in vain that you exert your empty voices on deaf ears, since they are unimpugned by the fact that they cannot hear. [5]For by nature they are deaf and dumb. [6]Therefore, the blame, in which justice is hidden, is yours since you are not willing to understand even that which you can see. [7]For the dense fog of error[C] which covers your eyes does not permit you to obtain the heavenly light which is the understanding of knowledge.[D]

55 [1]"Therefore, stay away from fabrications and creations which, as I have told you, are called 'gods' in name only, and are not gods by nature. [2]Rather, draw near to the one who by nature is God always and forever,[E] who was not fabricated, like your idols, nor was he created or formed like the images in which you

A. *what is the great altar . . . to devils*: Drijvers (*Cults and Beliefs*, 34–35) suggests that this great altar in the center of the city was still operating at the time when the storyteller compiled *Doctr. Addai*. This is plausible if *Doctr. Addai* was composed at the time of Rabbula, who instigated many anti-pagan policies, suggesting that there was still a good amount of paganism in Edessa at the beginning of the fifth century.

B. B continues here again. B reads "You who have eyes."

C. *dense fog of error*: the word "error" comes from the Syr. *ṭ'ā'* which refers to wandering or going astray. This is a classic term for heretics in Syriac literature and the root occurs in *Doctr. Addai* several times (cf. ch. 80 for a similar usage). For one's error blinding them see Wis 2:21; for light and enlightenment see John 12:40–46.

D. *the heavenly light which is the understanding of knowledge*: see a similar concept in Ephrem's *Eccl.* 36 and 37. There is no doubt that the writings of Ephrem were profoundly influential on the storyteller and community behind *Doctr. Addai.*

E. *by nature is God always and forever*: the use of "nature" (*kyānāyā*) echoes the language of the Council of Nicaea (325). The phrase "consubstantial with his Father" (*bār kyānāyā d'baw*) appears in the Syriac versions of the Nicene Creed. See Barnes, "'Nicene' Creed," 443.

glory. ³For although he put on this body, he is God along with his Father.^A ⁴For the creatures that trembled at his execution and were troubled by the suffering of his death testify that he is the one who created the creatures. ⁵It was not on behalf of a human being that the earth quaked, but on behalf of the one who spread out the earth upon the waters. ⁶Nor was it on behalf of a human being that the sun darkened at the cross, but on behalf of the one who made the great lights. ⁷Nor was it by a human being that the just and righteous were raised up, but by the one who gave authority over death from the beginning. ⁸Nor was it by a human being^B that the veil of the Jewish temple was rent from end to end, but by the one who said to them: 'See, your house is left desolate.'^C

Matt 27:51

Ps 136:6

Mark 15:33 par.

Ps 136:7

Matt 27:52–53

Mark 15:38 par.

Matt 23:38

56 ¹"For look: had those who crucified him not known that he was the Son of God, they would not have announced the ruin of their city, nor would they have caused sorrows to rain down upon themselves.^D ²Nor would they have surrendered themselves

A. *he is God along with his Father*: this statement is a clear Nicene christological sentiment that may also be taken in support of a miaphysite position. The use of *'apen* (=although) creates a contrary-to-fact statement, so contrary to the fact that he put on the body, Christ *is* God along with his Father. This idea combined with the earlier reference to his divine nature is suggestive of miaphysite Christology. The whole tenor of ch. 55, in fact, suggests a downplaying of Christ's humanity. See Griffith, "Doctrina Addai," 288–89.

B. *Nor was it by a human being*: Cyril of Alexandria writes to Nestorius: "[Christ] did not depart from his divine status or cease to be born of the Father; he continued to be what he was, even in taking on flesh" (*Ep.* 4; trans. from Norris, *Christological Controversies*, 134). The concern about the divinity of Jesus was important in Edessa's ecclesiastical politics beginning with the Nicene controversies of the councils of 325 and 381 in Constantinople. The Christians of Edessa and the surrounding regions were diverse in their opinions. The claims placed in the mouth of Addai in this speech are clearly designed to support particular positions of the storyteller and his community by projecting them back onto the first century. On the christological discussions of this period see Fiano, "Trinitarian Controversies."

C. *'See, your house is left desolate'*: the citation of Matt 23:38 (cf. Luke 13:35) is followed in Ephrem's commentary on the *Diatessaron* by the eschatological discourse, as it is thematically here. Addai's scriptural chronology thus once again appears to follow the *Diatessaron*.

D. *they would not have announced . . . down upon themselves*: a reference to the Jewish War and the destruction of Jerusalem and the Temple in 70 CE. This is yet another chronological error by the storyteller based on all of the other references to dates and figures thus far. The statement here specifically

to the great terrors that there were at that time, if they had not wished to admit acknowledgment of it. [3]For look, even some of the children of those who performed the crucifixion are today preachers and evangelists along with my fellow apostles, throughout all the land of Palestine, and among the Samaritans, and in all the country of the Philistines.[A] [4]All idols of the pagans are treated with contempt while the cross of Christ is honored, and peoples and creatures are confessing God who became a human being.

57 [1]"If indeed you believed in our Lord Jesus, that he is the Son of God, when he was on earth, and you confessed him to be God before you heard the word of his preaching, let no person among you have doubt in their mind, now that he has ascended to his Father and you have seen the signs and wonders which happen in his name and you have heard the gospel with your own ears, so that the promise of his blessing which he sent to you might be confirmed to you, namely, [2]"blessed are those who believe in me

John 20:29   although they have not seen me;[B] because you have thus believed in me, may the city in which you dwell be blessed and may no

---

implicates the Jews as being at fault for the war. Of course, from the storyteller's perspective, the culpability of the Jews is directly related to their role in the execution of Jesus. The earliest dated manuscript in any language, which was copied at Edessa in 411 (BL Add. 12150), contains a copy of Eusebius's *Theophania*, which gives a similar perspective to Addai here, including quotations from Josephus, *J.W.* 6, such as the Maria story where a woman in rebel-held Jerusalem cooks and eats her infant son. The Christians of Edessa in the early fifth century certainly knew these stories and the storyteller seems to have them in the back of his mind here.

A. *throughout all the land of Palestine . . . Samaritans . . . Philistines*: it is important that Addai only mentions evangelism in the Levant. The storyteller is attempting to create a link between Edessa and Palestine at the center of the origins of the Christian movement. The idea here is that Addai has come to Edessa *before* any of the other apostles went into Asia Minor and Europe. From the standpoint of the storyteller, Christianity spreads outward from Jerusalem, then to Edessa, and then everywhere else.

B. *blessed are those . . .* : a reference to Jesus' words in his reply to Abgar. See ch. 5 above. Addai's appeal here mirrors Jesus' words to Abgar: the audience was not in Jerusalem to witness Jesus in person, they are vicarious witnesses through the miracles and teaching of Addai. Nevertheless, just as Jesus pronounced blessings on Abgar for believing without seeing, so here Addai pronounces blessings on the audience for doing the same.

enemy ever have authority over it."[A] [3]Therefore, do not depart from his faith. [4]For, look, you have heard and seen those things which testify to his faith, that he is the august Son and glorious God, the invincible king, the mighty force. [5]By his true faith a person can acquire the eye of a true mind[B] and understand that the wrath of justice will tread upon anyone who worships created things.

58 [1]"Everything that we are saying before you, we say, teach, and show just as we received from the favor of our Lord so that you might obtain your lives[C] and not destroy your spirits by the deceit of paganism. [2]For heavenly light has dawned on creation. [3]This is the one who chose the ancestors of old, the upright and the prophets, and spoke with them by means of revelation of the Spirit of Holiness. [4]For he is the God of the very Jews who crucified him. [5]Though they do not know it, the erring pagans worship him also, because there is no other God in heaven or on earth. [6]And look: thanksgiving goes up to him from the four quarters of the earth. [7]Therefore, look: your ears have now heard what you have not heard before, and again, your eyes have seen what they have never seen before. [8]Therefore, do not be deniers in light of what you have heard and seen.

cf. Matt 4:16

cf. Heb 1:1

cf. Acts 17:22–34

A. *may no enemy ever have authority over it*: or "may the enemy [i.e., Satan] never have authority over it." See the note in ch. 5.

B. *the eye of a true mind*: the expression appears also in chs. 80 and 84. This could have philosophical overtones related to Neoplatonic philosophy. Bardaisan and his followers had ties to Neoplatonic thought. However, we cannot rule out other influences, such as Ephrem's symbolic use of the eyes in his hymns. In *Eccl.* 37 Ephrem writes: "Through the eye that was darkened | the whole world has darkened, and people groped | and through that every stone they stumbled upon was a god | calling falsehood truth. But when it was illumined by the other eye, | and the heavenly light | that resided in its midst, | humanity became reconciled once again, | realizing that what they had stumbled on | was destroying their very life" (trans. from Brock, *Luminous Eye*, 72–73). This stanza parallels Addai's speech quite nicely and is contextually relevant with the mention of other gods and the "falsehood" of paganism.

C. *your lives*: or "your salvation." Jesus promised that his emissary would "turn all who are with you toward eternal life." The word for "life" (*ḥaye*) can carry the symbolic weight of *the* life, eternal life/salvation.

59 [1]"Remove the insolent mind of your ancestors[A] from yourselves and free yourselves from the yoke of sin which rules over you in the form of libations and sacrifices before images.[B] [2]Attend to your perishing lives and your vain idolatry.[C] [3]Rather, obtain a new mind, one that worships the maker and not the made, (a mind) in which is depicted the image of rightness and truth[D] of the Father and the Son and the Spirit of Holiness when you believe and are baptized into the three glorious names.[E]

A. *insolent mind of your ancestors*: the appeal to reject ancestral worship is doubly levied at the storyteller's actual audience as well as the fictive audience of Addai. The storyteller is attempting to rewrite the ancestry of the Edessene nobility throughout the narrative. He represents the ancestors of his actual audience as correctly rejecting their pagan past, even while asking his audience to do the very same thing.

B. *libations and sacrifices before images*: libations and sacrifices are similarly targeted in *Hist. John*, making this a likely central theme in the religious polemics of the storyteller's time. As Drijvers (*Cults and Beliefs*) shows, sacrificial religions were still quite prominent in northern Mesopotamia in the late fourth and early fifth centuries. The focus on dismantling these cults in the face of a growing Christian presence reinforces the likelihood that *Doctr. Addai* was written especially for this propagandistic purpose.

C. *your vain idolatry*: Syr. *markan rīškōn bṭīlā*. cf. Payne-Smith, *Compendious Syriac Dictionary*, 542.

D. *the image of rightness and truth*: in contrast to the physical images being worshiped by the Edessenes, Addai invokes a symbolic "image" in the mind. Steiner (*Images in Mind*) demonstrates that poets and philosophers used images of gods/goddesses to think with, pondering the relationship between an original and its copy. A similar idea may be operative here, only Addai is urging his audience to reject any notion of a copy and turn toward an internal image of the original.

E. *baptized into the three glorious names*: this is the first call to baptism in the narrative (though it is mentioned in the citation of Matt 28 in ch. 40 above). Baptism is the central theme of *Hist. John* but does not play as central a role in *Doctr. Addai*. The appearance of both narratives in A may have been intended as a multi-faceted attack against religious practices that the scribes of the manuscript deemed dangerous or inauthentic. The lack of attention to baptism as a rite in *Doctr. Addai* may reflect an early stage of Christianity in Edessa in which a full baptismal ritual was still in development. On the Syrian baptismal rite, see Brock, "Syrian Orthodox Baptismal Liturgy"; and Klijn, "Ancient Syriac Baptismal Liturgy."

60 [1]"This, therefore, is our teaching and our preaching.[A] [2]For it is not by many means that the truth of Christ is made credible; and those of you who wish to be instructed by Christ know that I have repeated my words many times before you so that you may learn and understand everything you hear. [3]And just as the ploughman rejoices[B] in his field which is blessed, so we rejoice and our God[C] is glorified by your penitence to him. [4]Since it is in this you have life, so we who have counseled you in this will not be cheated in its blessed wages.

61 [1]"Because I am confident that you are a blessed land,[D] according to the will of the Lord Christ, for this reason, instead of the dust of my feet, which we were told to shake off upon the town who does not receive our words, look: [2]today I shake off at the gate of your ears the words of my lips by which are prefigured[E] the coming of Christ, which has happened and will happen; the resurrection and revival of all humanity; the separation that is between believers and infidels;[F] and the blessed promise of joy that is to come, which those who believe in Christ and worship him and his exalted Father and have confessed him and the Spirit of his divinity shall receive.

Mark 6:11 par.

A. *This, therefore, is our teaching and our preaching*: it is not clear what the singular demonstrative pronoun "this" (Syr. *hādā*) refers to, whether it goes back to the immediate context of believe and be baptized, from the previous line, or if it is meant to refer to Addai's entire speech up to this point.

B. *rejoices*: only B has "rejoices." I have supplied it here to complete the sense of the verse.

C. *our God*: B only has "God."

D. *a blessed land*: Edessa later came to be known as the "blessed city," in no small part due to Jesus' promise in his letter to Abgar that the city would never be ruled by enemies. This status is conferred upon Edessa via the specific addition of Jesus' blessing which first appears in *Doctr. Addai* (though it is referred to by Egeria).

E. *by which are prefigured*: B has the active participle instead of the passive participle.

F. *between believers and infidels*: B adds the phrase: "and the severe punishment that is reserved for those who do not know God." Illert (*Doctrina Addai*, 158 n. 62) suggests that this statement is reminiscent of polemical statements against Origen's doctrine of universal salvation. It is possible that the scribe who added this phrase was familiar with Origenist polemics.

[3]"Now, it is fitting for us to end our current speech. [4]Those who have received the message of Christ, as well as those who wish to join with us in prayer, let them remain by our side. [5]Then let them go to their homes."

The Success of Addai's Preaching

62 [1]The apostle Addai rejoiced in that he saw the great number of citizens remained with him and there were few of those who did not stay with him at that time. [2]And even those few received his words after a few days and they believed in the good news of the message of Christ.

[3]After the apostle Addai had spoken these things in front of the whole city of Urhay, King Abgar saw that the whole city rejoiced because of his teaching—men and women together—and were saying to him, "Christ who sent you to us is true and faithful!" And Abgar also rejoiced greatly in this, praising God, for just as he had heard from Ḥannan his archivist about Christ, so now he saw the astonishing powers the apostle Addai performed in the name of Christ.

63 [1]King Abgar also said to Addai, "Just as I sent to Christ in my letter[A] to him, and just as he also sent to me and I have received from you today, so now I shall believe all the days of my life.[B] [2]In

A. *letter*: A has the *seyame* over the word indicating that it is plural, while B does not, though such indicators in early manuscripts can be very inconsistent.

B. *so now I shall believe all the days of my life*: Abgar's confession here brings to mind the passing statement of Bardaisan of Edessa in his *Bk. Laws* that "when King Abgar believed" (*wkad haymen abgār malkā*), the practice of genital mutilation was outlawed (trans. Drijvers, *Book of the Laws of Countries*, 58–59). If this reference is an original part of Bardaisan's work, then it would refer to Abgar VIII, the Great (reg. 177–212 CE), the same Abgar who was king during the great flood of 201. It is not clear, however, what this statement actually means. Some have taken it as an indication that Abgar VIII was the first Edessene monarch to convert to Christianity (see Burkitt, *Early Eastern Christianity*; Duval, *Histoire politique*; Segal, *Edessa*; and Ross, *Roman Edessa*). This is not impossible, though Brock ("Eusebius," 223–24) has raised the problem that in his quotation of Bardaisan's work, Eusebius fails to mention that Abgar "believed," suggesting that the statement was not in the earliest version of Bardaisan's work. This is difficult to reconcile, though Ross

these very things I shall remain while I boast, for I know that there is no other power in whose name these signs and marvels happen, but by the power of Christ whom you proclaim in justice and in truth. ³Therefore, I and my son Ma'nu,ᴬ and Augustina, and Queen Šalmath shall worship him.

64 ¹"Therefore, build a church,ᴮ a meeting place, wherever you wish,ᶜ for those who have believed and will believe in your words. ²And just as you were commanded by your Lord, you shall assuredly serve at times and I am prepared to give great giftsᴰ to those who will become teachers of this gospel with you, so that they might not need other work than the affairs of ministry. ³I shall give to you without endᴱ everything that you require for the

points out that since Eusebius had already told the story of Abgar Ukkāmā converting in the first century, it would have created a problem of continuity to subsequently claim "*when* Abgar believed," as if the Abgarids had not already accepted Christianity from Thaddaeus. In other words, Eusebius simply omitted the statement from his quotation of Bardaisan.

A. *Ma'nu*: see ch. 100 which mentions "sons" of Abgar. Here, Abgar only mentions one son. *Chron. Zuq.* 97–98 mentions that in 53 CE "Ma'nu son of Abgar, king of Edessa, died, and his brother Ma'nu reigned for fourteen years" (trans. Harrak, *Chronicle of Zuqnīn*, 160–63). The chronology could work, if the chronicle has Abgar Ukkāmā in mind, who reigned until 50 CE. This would mean that his first son reigned only for three years and his other son, of the same name, took over. The storyteller has made several historical blunders to this point, but may have had access to official civic records which would allow for a more convincing chronology of the Edessene rulers. See the note in ch. 100.

B. *build a church*: the "church of the Christians" is mentioned in *Chron. Ed.* (Guidi, *Chronica Minora I*, 1–2). It was damaged in the flood of 201 CE. The mention of a church in Edessa already in the early third century has been taken as further evidence that the legend of Abgar extends back to Abgar VIII the Great.

C. *you wish*: A has the verb *tsbā* (to wish, want, desire) and B has *b'ā* (to seek, desire).

D. *I am prepared to give great gifts*: Abgar's wish to give gifts is consistently denied by Addai and his successors (see chs. 13, 93, 97). Addai (ch. 53) and his successors (ch. 99) are careful not to compel people by force or bribery to convert.

E. *without end*: Syr. *dlā ḥušbān*. B has *dlā ḥušāb* "without reckoning." Both terms have to do with the numbering or calculating of funds or resources. The idea in both is the same: Abgar is giving Addai unfettered access to whatever resources he needs for the building of the church—both physically and

expenses of building, for it is your word, and no one else's, that has authority and reigns in this city. [4]You shall enter before me freely into the palace which is the honor of my kingdom."[A]

65 [1]After King Abgar[B] had gone down to his royal palace, he rejoiced along with his nobles—'Abdu,[C] Garmai, Šmešgrām,[D] Abubai, and Meherdeth,[E] along with their other companions—in everything their eyes had seen and their ears had heard. [2]And with rejoicing in their heart they praised God, who had turned their mind to him as they renounced the paganism in which they lived and acknowledged the gospel of Christ. [3]After Addai built the church, the nobles and the people of the city were offering votives and oblations in it and were serving there all the days of their lives.[F]

----

spiritually.

A. *the palace which is the honor of my kingdom*: Abgar's palace is mentioned in several texts and the remnants of it still survive today (Segal, *Edessa*, 24–27). This palace was built after the flood of 201 CE that is recorded in *Chron. Ed.* Segal indicates that this palace was probably located at the Southwestern end of the city on the Citadel mount. After the flood, Abgar VIII reportedly acted quickly to reorganize the city watch, which did little to prevent future floods. Far more effective, it seems, was his move to relocate the palace and the houses of the nobility to well above the floodline.

B. *King Abgar*: B omits "King."

C. *'Abdu*: B adds "bar 'Abdu" who is mentioned also in chs. 7, 14, and 24.

D. *Šmešgrām*: see chs. 1, 2, 33, and 35. This nobleman is consistently mentioned, along with 'Abdu bar 'Abdu, among the nobility of King Abgar. The other names here are new and the narrative has seen a number of different names of the Edessene nobility appear throughout. Probably the consistent names were those of the greatest importance who wished to have their family's legacy inscribed in the history of Edessa's conversion to Christianity.

E. *Meherdeth*: B has the spelling "Mehdreth," transposing the *dāleth* and the *riš*. This is not an uncommon problem in early Syriac manuscripts as the practice of adding dots to letters was still developing as a scribal habit.

F. *the nobles . . . all the days of their lives*: the specific mention of the nobles giving their offerings and service for their whole lives perhaps hints at the interests in the nobility to be represented as strong supporters of the church from its beginnings. Since this narrative was composed after the monarchy was dissolved, it is the descendants of the nobility who had the most to gain from this narrative. Saint-Laurent (*Missionary Stories*, 44) is correct in saying that the storytellers of *Doctr. Addai* "create enmity with their imagined Christian ancestors in the past" with the representations of Jews and "pagans"

66 [1]Then ʿAwidā and Bar Kalbā, who were chiefs and commanders and who wore royal tiaras,[A] drew near to Addai and asked Addai about the subject of Christ, that he might tell them how, although he was God, he had appeared to them like a human being and how it was possible to see him.[B] [2]He satisfied them about this, about all that their eyes had seen and about everything that their ears had heard from him. [3]And he narrated to them everything that the prophets had said about him and they received his words with gladness and faith. [4]No one stood against him, for the exploits he performed permitted no one to stand against him.[C]

in the city; however, they also create *continuity* between their own time and the imagined past, and thus between the nobility of their own day and centuries earlier. See also Castelli, *Martyrdom and Memory*, 30–32 on this idea of myth.

A. *tiaras*: this is reading *ḥude* with a *dāleth*, which is found in B. In A, the letter has no dot and could also be *ḥewāre*, "white garments." The reading of B is probably better in this case since the same term appears in ch. 68 with reference to Aggai as a maker of "royal silks and tiaras." On ʿAwidā see the note in ch. 35. On Bar Kalbā see the note in ch. 33.

B. *how it was possible to see him*: A suddenly shifts to direct discourse: "How was it possible for you to see him?" B stays with indirect discourse, which has the more natural flow. *although he was God . . . possible to see him*: this question about the divinity and humanity of Jesus was central to the christological debates, beginning with Arius in the early fourth century and up through the fifth century debates that led to the councils of Ephesus (431 CE) and Chalcedon (451 CE).

C. *No one stood against him . . . stand against him*: commenting on the primacy of Addai and his gospel. The reference to ʿAwidā here becomes more evident as a symbol of Addai's triumph over Bardaisan's gospel, and thus the storyteller's group and their perceived triumph over Bardaisanite Christians of their time.

67 [1]Now, Šawida[A] and ʿAbednebo,[B] chief priests of this city, along with their fellows Peroz[C] and Denqu,[D] when they saw the wonders Addai performed, ran and tore down the altars upon which they made sacrifices before their gods Nebo and Bel[E]— with the exception of the great altar in the middle of the city.[F] [2]And they were shouting and saying, "Truly this is the disciple of that skilled and glorious teacher of whom we have heard everything that he did in the land of Palestine." [3]Addai received all those who believed in Christ and baptized them in the name of the Father and the Son and the Spirit of Holiness. [4]Those who had worshiped rocks and trees were sitting at his feet learning and receiving correction from the raging madness of paganism. [5]Even the Jews, the discerners of the Law and the Prophets, who

cf. Matt 28:19

A. *Šawida*: this variant of the earlier name ʿAwidā occurs only here.

B. *ʿAbednebo*: lit. 'servant of Nebo.' This name is reminiscent of "Sharbel" from *Mart. Sharb.*, whose name is an amalgam of Ishtar and Bel. The name ʿAbednebo is a play on the thematic concept of a servant of Nebo destroying the cultic shrines to Nebo.

C. *Peroz*: Persian "victorious." This name also has significant connections to the Manichaeans, since it was a certain Peroz who, near the end of the third century, recommended Mani to King Shapur. The symbolism behind the name is similar to that of Addai: the important figures in Manichaean history are recalibrated as Christian figures of the same group as the storyteller. See the note in Desreumaux, *Histoire*, 129.

D. *Denqu*: possibly a cognate of *denaq*, "to torment."

E. *tore down the altars . . . Nebo and Bel*: the downfall of the "pagan" cults in Edessa is symbolic of the downfall of these same cults in the storyteller's time. Their Christianity triumphs over any native cults and cultic practice. *Mart. Sharb.* has a similar idea expressed, but here there is no mention of a Sharbel, confirming that the martyr legend is in fact later than *Doctr. Addai*.

F. *with the exception of the great altar in the middle of the city*: Drijvers ("Persistence of Pagan Cults," 38–40) suggests that, in fact, pagan altars and shrines still stood in the city center at the time of *Doctr. Addai*'s composition. Illert (*Doctrina Addai*, 160 n. 64) notes that the tearing down of a "pagan" altar is consistent with the Theodotian edicts of the late fourth and early fifth century (*Cod. Theod.* 16.10.3). Bishop Rabbula's *Comm. Admon.* also admonishes monks, priests, and members of *bnay/bnat qyāmā* for associating with "heretics." See Phenix and Horn, *Rabbula Corpus*, 101, 115. *Comm. Admon.* 53 instructs: "If the remainder of a temple of idols stands in the place, let it be torn down quietly without disturbance." The mention of this existing altar by Addai may have served to reinforce Rabbula's own directives to remove such structures.

sold silks, even they were persuaded and became disciples and confessed Christ, that he is the Son of the living God. [6]But neither King Abgar nor the apostle Addai compelled anyone by force to believe in Christ.[A] [7]Because it was not by the force of a human being, but the force of signs that compelled many to believe in him.[B] [8]And this whole region of Mesopotamia, as well as all the regions surrounding it, received his teaching with love.[C]

68 [1]Then Aggai,[D] who made royal silks and tiaras, Palūt,[E]

A. *But neither King Abgar . . . by force to believe in Christ*: once again, as in ch. 53, the storyteller insists that no one was compelled to convert.

B. *it was not by force*: this statement is reminiscent of John 1:13 in regard to the incarnation of the Word. It was "not of blood or of the will of the flesh or of the will of man" that the Word was born, but by the will of God. A similar idea seems to be at work here.

C. *Mesopotamia, as well as all the regions surrounding it*: Addai does not leave Edessa, according to *Doctr. Addai*, but his followers carry his gospel outside of Mesopotamia and into "Assyria" (see ch. 72). In *Teach. Apos.* 6:9–10, Addai is said to have converted Edessa, Nisibis, Arabia, and all of Mesopotamia. According to the same text, Aggai converted Persia, Assyria, the land of the Arameans, the Medes, Babylon, the Huzites, and the Gilanians, to the borders of India, and as far as Gog and Magog. *Acts Mārī* claims that Addai converted all of Mesopotamia and that Mār Marī converted the various regions of Assyria and Babylonia (see Harrak, *Acts of Mār Mārī*, 11 n. 18).

D. *Aggai*: Eusebius does not mention Aggai, though he does appear in *Teach. Apos.* as Addai's immediate successor. There he is also said to be a maker of silks. This connection strengthens the literary relationship between *Doctr. Addai* and *Teach. Apos.*

E. *Palūt*: the name Palūt undoubtedly conjures up the bishop of Edessa from the early fourth century, after whom Ephrem says the pro-Nicene faction of Christians in the city named themselves (*Haer.* 22.5–6). In ch. 102, Palūt is in fact ordained bishop after the murder of Aggai, Addai's immediate successor. Bauer (*Orthodoxy and Heresy*, 17–20) makes a great deal of the possible connections between this literary figure and the historical Palūt. If indeed the same person is meant by the storyteller, this would be an egregious anachronism by several hundred years and it is hard to believe hearers would have found it very convincing. It is likely that the name is symbolic in the context of *Doctr. Addai*. This Palūt, just like his later namesake, was a faithful bishop who followed in the line of Addai.

'Abšelāmā,[A] and Barsmayā,[B] along with the rest of their fellows, followed the apostle Addai and, receiving them, Addai made them participants with him in ministry. [2]They were reading in the Old Covenant and the New, and in the Prophets and in the Acts of the Apostles, meditating on them daily.[C]

A. *Abšelāmā*: this figure appears only here among the first leaders of the church ordained by Addai. The name is found in a cave inscription south of the citadel, from the second or third century CE (Drijvers, *Old Syriac Inscriptions*, no. 52). It was probably a name attached to a noble family, or at least one that offered verisimilitude for the storyteller of *Doctr. Addai*.

B. *Barsmayā*: this character makes appearances in *Mart. Sharb.* as the successor of Palūt as bishop of Edessa, and in his own martyrdom account, *Mart. Bars.* This strengthens the connections between these three narratives. Barsmayā appears alongside other nobility of Edessa, including 'Awidā, Bar Kalbā, and Ḥaphsai, in *Doctr. Addai* and in these two martyrdom cycles. These martyr acts, according to Camplani ("Traditions," 268), served to confer "authority upon the Edessene nobility, attributing to it an ancient case of martyrdom."

C. *the Old Covenant . . . the Acts of the Apostles*: this reveals something of the state of the Bible in the East at the time of the composition of *Doctr. Addai*. A similar statement found in *Teach. Apos.* says that "the apostles decreed that except the Old Testament, the Prophets, the Gospel, and the Acts of their Heroic Deeds, nothing more should be read on the *bema* of the church" (3:10 trans. Witakowski, *MNTA*). The omission of Paul's letters here is conspicuous, especially since they are mentioned as accepted writings in ch. 88. This list here, however, need not imply that the pro-Nicene faction responsible for *Doctr. Addai* were anti Paul or that they rejected his letters. This list is more likely commenting on texts used for liturgical purposes, which would include readings from the Old Testament, the Psalms, and the Gospel, followed by a *memrā* or verse homily. The silence on Paul's letters here thus may not be a comment on the development of the Syriac biblical canon as much as it is a comment on the state of the liturgy (see Desreumaux, *Histoire*, 96 n. 150). Another puzzle here is the identification of the "acts of the apostles." To what text(s) does this refer? The Syriac phrase *šō'rānayhōn d'ašliḥe* is the same phrase found in the passage from *Teach. Apos.* However, in ch. 88 it is the *praksis* (πράξις) *d'tr'esar šliḥe* that are to be read before the church. It is possible that these two alternative titles refer to the same book: the canonical Acts of the Apostles. Both titles are used in Syriac literature with reference to the canonical book. However, if we look at the contexts, the present passage seems to refer to broad collections of texts—Old Testament, New Testament, the Prophets—whereas in ch. 88 we have specific mention of the Law, the Prophets, the Gospel, and the Letters of Paul. It is possible that in the present passage the *šō'rānayhon d'šliḥe* refers to various acts of apostles, perhaps even *Doctr. Addai* itself. Egeria (*Itin.* 19.2) says that she read from the writings of St. Thomas while at Edessa and this may very well have been the *Acts of*

69 [1]He was commanding them carefully, "Let your flesh be clean and your bodies[A] be sanctified as is fitting for people who stand before the altar of God," and be "far removed from vain oaths, from impious killing, from false testimony—which is mingled with adultery—from enchantments upon which there is no mercy; [2]from auguries and divinations and spirits of the dead, from lot casting and horoscopes, in which the erring Chaldeans boast, and from stars and signs of the Zodiac in which fools trust. [3]Put away from you the appearance of lawlessness, bribes, and gifts by which the innocent are convicted.[B]

70 [1]"And along with this ministry to which you have been called, you should not again have another occupation, for the Lord is the occupation of your ministry all the days of your life. [2]You should take pains to give the sign of baptism; you should not desire the possessions of this world; you should listen to judgement with uprightness and truth. [3]You should not be a stumbling block to the blind, lest the name of the one who opened the eyes of the blind—just as we have seen[C]—be reviled among you. [4]Therefore, whosoever sees you will perceive that you follow everything which you preach and teach."

71 [1]So they ministered with Addai in the church that he built by the word and order of King Abgar, being provided for by the king

---

Thomas. One is tempted to also include other acts among those that could have been read from the very same manuscript in which we find *Doctr. Addai*, including *Hist. Sim. Ceph.* and *Hist. John.* We should allow for the possibility that the storytellers behind the copies of *Doctr. Addai* were familiar with multiple acts of apostles being read often in the liturgical context.

A. *Let your flesh be clean and your bodies be sanctified*: this phrase is indirect discourse in A. I follow B here which places it and the following lines in direct discourse.

B. *far removed from vain oaths . . . by which the innocent are convicted*: the directives in this chapter are reminiscent of the *Commandments and Admonitions for the Priests and Children of the Covenant* in the Rabbula corpus. Rabbula repeatedly denies priests from being involved in any kind of financial transactions with people and specifically forbids interactions with diviners and charmers (canon 17). See Phenix and Horn, *Rabbula Corpus*, 102–17.

C. *just as we have seen*: a reference to Abgar's letter to Jesus, that Abgar had heard of Jesus' healing the blind (above in ch. 4:3).

and his nobles.[A] [2]They brought some things for the house of God and some things for the care of the poor.[B] [3]Then many people were assembling daily and coming for the prayer service, of the Old Covenant, and the New of the *Diatessaron*.[C] [4]They believed in the resurrection of the dead and buried their departed ones in the hope of the resurrection. [5]They observed the church festivals

A. *the king and his nobles*: yet another reference to the involvement of the Edessene nobility in the founding of Christianity in the city. In this case, *Doctr. Addai* makes the explicit connection between the nobility and the first church building in the city, constructed by Addai at the behest of King Abgar, and funded by both Abgar and his nobility. The verb here, *parnes*, implies having management over something, or supplying something with sustenance, in this case monetary sustenance. The nobility not only furnish the church, but they also provide for the poor of the city.

B. *the care of the poor*: care for the poor is an essential feature in Rabbula's *Comm. Admon.* 11, 12, 16, 24, 34.

C. *the Diatessaron*: the *Diatessaron* may have been composed in Syriac by Tatian in the second century. It remained the primary form of the Gospels for the Syriac churches until the early fifth century when bishop Rabbula ordered the adoption of the four separate Gospels. The promotion of the *Diatessaron* here is thus of crucial importance for dating *Doctr. Addai*. If the storyteller is advocating for the use of the *Diatessaron* in the church of Edessa, then this may mean that *Doctr. Addai* dates prior to Rabbula's order to have the four separate Gospels translated into Syriac. However, support for the *Diatessaron* could also indicate that the storyteller stands in opposition to Rabbula's order and instead believe that the *Diatessaron* represented a more ancient, authentic, and distinctly Edessene form of the Gospels. The *Diatessaron* was used by the Nicene faction of Christianity in Edessa. Ephrem the Syrian wrote a commentary on it, which survives only in Armenian translation apart from various fragments. We can assume, therefore, that the Christians who used the *Diatessaron* were those of Ephrem's ilk, or Nicenes. It is possible that this group, having secured the dominant position in the late fourth and early fifth centuries under the brutal suppression of other religious rivals at the instigation of Rabbula, had split due to the decisions of the Council of Ephesus in 431. The see of Antioch supported Nestorius in the matter and Edessa fell under the jurisdiction of Antioch. Rabbula, however, became a staunch supporter of Cyril of Alexandria and after this point came into conflict with Hiba (Ibas), the director of the School of the Persians, who supported Nestorius and his teacher Theodore of Mopsuestia. Eventually, this inter-Nicene rivalry would result in the School being moved to Nisibis under the dyophysite leader Narsai, while Edessa would become a center of miaphysitism. *Doctr. Addai* could thus stand at the cusp of this split. The support of using the *Diatessaron* in church could be seen in opposition to Rabbula's regime of propagating the Alexandrian, miaphysite position. See Phenix and Horn, *Rabbula Corpus*, 113.

in their appointed times and every day they remained constant in the church vigils.[A] [6]They made visitations of alms to the sick and the healthy, according to Addai's teaching to them.

72 [1]In the places surrounding the city, churches were built and many people received the hand of the priesthood from (Addai).[B] [2]Moreover, people from the east passed over into Roman territory in the likeness of merchants in order to see the wonders Addai performed and those among them who became disciples received the hand of the priesthood from him and made disciples of their people's children in their own land of Assyria.[C] [3]They made houses of prayer there in secret out of fear of fire worshipers and those who honor fire.[D]

73 [1]Then Narseh,[E] king of the Assyrians, sent to King Abgar when he heard about the things the apostle Addai had done:

A. *constant in the church vigils*: canon 27 of Rabbula's directives to priests and the *qyāmā* states: "The priests, the deacons, the sons of the covenant, and the daughters of the covenant shall be constant in the service of the church and shall not forsake the times of prayer and the [singing of] psalms by night and by day" (trans. from Phenix and Horn, *Rabbula Corpus*, 109).

B. *hand of the priesthood*: See the note on this phrase in the prologue. This statement positions Addai and Edessa at the center of Christian expansion in Mesopotamia, arguably the primary strategy for the storyteller of *Doctr. Addai.*

C. *Assyria*: Syr. *āthūrāye*. Grk. Ἀσσούρ. Once again, *Doctr. Addai* makes a claim that Edessa lies at the center of Christian expansion to the East. In all likelihood, there were Christians already in these regions prior to its taking root in Edessa. See Taylor, "Coming of Christianity."

D. *fire worshipers and those who honor fire*: that is, Zoroastrians, the primary cult of the Sassanian Empire during the fourth and fifth centuries. Eusebius records a great persecution that broke out against Sassanian Christians after the conversion of Constantine and numerous accounts of Persian martyrs have survived that purport to document persecutions. Some of these accounts appear to contain authentic details while others are purely fictional. Only recently has some light begun to be shed on the early history of Christianity in Sassanian regions. See especially Smith, *Constantine*; and Payne, *State of Mixture*. B appears to have "water" in place of the second "fire."

E. *Narseh*: Narseh, the third son of Shapur I, ruled the Sassanians from 293–302. See González Núñez, *Leyenda*, 73; and Jullien, *Apôtres des confines*, 216. This is another serious anachronism but may indicate something of the storyteller's image of the Roman world, which only goes back about a century earlier than *Doctr. Addai*'s final form. Narseh declared war on Rome in 296

[2]"Either send to me the man who performed these wonders in your presence so that I might see him and hear his message, or send along (an account) of all the things you have seen him perform in your city." [3]So Abgar wrote to Narseh and informed him of the whole story of the matter of Addai from beginning to end. He did not omit anything in what he wrote to him. [4]When Narseh heard what was written to him he was amazed and marveled.

The Letter from Abgar to Tiberius

74 [1]Then, because King Abgar was not able to pass over into Roman territory and enter into Palestine and kill the Jews on account of their crucifying Christ, he wrote a letter and sent it to Tiberius Caesar,[A] writing as follows:

[2]"King Abgar to our lord Tiberius Caesar: greeting.[B] [3]While I know that nothing is hidden from your majesty, I write to you and make known to your powerful and great authority, that the Jews under your dominion who dwell in the land of Palestine have gathered together and crucified Christ, who was undeserving of

---

due to Rome's meddling in Armenia. He defeated Diocletian and Galerius near Ḥārrān in that year, but was unable to hold control and made a treaty with Rome in 297/298. Part of this treaty allowed more Roman control over Armenia and Hiberia/Iberia. This conflict may be what the storyteller had in mind with reference to Tiberius and the Hiberians/Iberians in ch. 16. This would mean that Ramelli's theory (see above pg. 46) is partially correct: the storyteller did, in fact, have the Hiberians/Iberians in mind rather than the Spaniards, but instead of the historical conflict between Tiberius in this region, the storyteller evokes the more recent events of the Roman Tetrarchy's conflict with the Sassanians over control of the area. This would further explain why *Doctr. Addai* seems to assume a tetrarchy of Roman rulers by mentioning Tiberius, Claudius, and Gaius.

A. *he wrote a letter and sent it to Tiberius Caesar*: such a correspondence is not impossible, though we have no official record of it outside of *Doctr. Addai*. Ramelli ("Possible Historical Traces") defends the possibility that such letters existed and were plausibly contained in the civic archives of Edessa where *Doctr. Addai* purportedly was held along with the letters of Abgar and Jesus. Moses of Chorene, a later Armenian historian of debatable trustworthiness, attests to the existence of letters between Abgar Ukkāmā and Tiberius and even cites an additional letter not included in *Doctr. Addai*.

B. *greeting*: lacking in B.

death, after having performed signs and wonders in front of them and showing them mighty powers and signs.[A] [4]Moreover, he even gave life to the dead. At the moment they crucified him the sun went dark and the earth quaked and all creatures trembled, and as if for their part,[B] all creation and its inhabitants ceased at this affair. [5]Therefore, your majesty knows what is the right thing to command concerning the people of the Jews who have done these things."

Mark 15:33–51 par.

75 [1]Then Tiberius Caesar wrote and sent to King Abgar and wrote to him as follows:

[2]"I have received your sincere letter to me and it was read to me, concerning every deed which the Jews committed[C] with regard to the cross. [3]Moreover, the procurator Pilate wrote and made known to Aulbinus my governor[D] about these matters which you have written to me. [4]On account of my war taking place right now with the Spaniards,[E] who have rebelled against me, I am not able to look into this matter. [5]But I am prepared to make a legal charge against the Jews, who have acted illegally, whenever I have a reprieve. [6]Moreover, on the matter of Pilate, who was appointed my procurator there, I have appointed another in his place[F] and I have dismissed (Pilate) in disgrace, because he abandoned the law and acted according to the will of the Jews and for the sake of the Jews crucified Christ—who, based

A. *and signs*: lacking in B.

B. *for their part*: *wayk dmen ṭsedayhun*. A strange phrase in Syriac. See Payne-Smith, *Compendious Syriac Dictionary*, 477.

C. *committed*: Syr. *sʿar*. B has the verb *sʿā*, "to dare" or "to presume."

D. *Aulbinus my governor*: that is Albinus, who replaced Festus as governor to Judaea (Josephus, *A.J.* 20.197; Eusebius *Hist. eccl.* 2.23.21). As Cureton (*Ancient Syriac Documents*, 160) notes, this is probably meant to refer to Vitellius, whom Tiberius appointed to replace Pilate. See the note below. Albinus is also mentioned in *Hist. Sim. Ceph.* 30 (and *Acts Pet.* 34) as a friend of the emperor, and whose wife, Xanthippe, becomes a follower of Peter.

E. *Spaniards*: Syr. *bnay ʾespnyʾa*. On this conflict with the Spaniards see the notes in chs. 16 and 71.

F. *I have appointed another in his place*: Tiberius did in fact replace Pilate with Lucius Vitellius, whom Tiberius appointed governor of Syria in 35 CE. Josephus, *A.J.* 18.4.3 records that Vitellius wrote to Tiberius requesting that the high priestly robe be given back to the Jews to do with as they pleased.

on what I hear about him, instead of a cross of death, he ought[A] to be honored. [7]It is fitting that he should be worshiped by them, especially since they saw with their own eyes everything that he did.[B] [8]Now as for you, in accordance with your loyalty to me and the faithful covenant of yours and your fathers, you have done well in writing to me in this way."

76 [1]King Abgar received Aristides,[C] who had been sent to him from Tiberius Caesar and (Abgar) returned (Aristides) and sent him (back) with gifts of honor that befit the one who sent (Aristides) to him. And he went forth[D] from Urhay and he came to Tiqnutha[E] where Claudius, the king's second in command, was. [2]From there he went to Artiqa[F] where Tiberius Caesar was, while

A. *he ought*: B lacks this verb, which would render the sense awkward. It is possible that the scribe of B misunderstood the verb *wāle* for the negative particle with a conjunction *wlā*. In fact, Howard (*Teaching of Addai*, 78–79) took this as a negative particle as well, even though there is a diacritical dot above the word suggesting it should be taken as a participle.

B. *since they saw . . . everything that he did*: in contrast to Abgar and the Edessenes, who believed without seeing, the Jews saw and did not believe. This polemic against the Jews is quite common in literature of this period. This contrast further enhances the primacy of Edessa, even vis-à-vis Jerusalem. Those who lived in Jerusalem and saw Jesus perform his miracles did not believe in him, whereas the Edessenes, who did not witness with their own eyes, did believe.

C. *Aristides*: only mentioned here, serving as a courier between Abgar and Tiberius. In 76:3 Aristides is said to have recounted Addai's story before Tiberius. Eusebius (*Hist. eccl.* 4.3.3) mentions an apology written by an Aristides addressed to the emperor Hadrian. A Syriac translation of Aristides' apology to Hadrian was discovered by J. Rendel Harris in a seventh century manuscript from St. Catherine's Monastery at Mount Sinai (syr. 16). It is possible that the storyteller knew of this apology and its delivery before a Roman emperor and thus used the name Aristides, but placed him during the reign of Tiberius in order to fit his chronology.

D. *And he went forth*: B lacks this verb.

E. *Tiqnutha*: B has the spelling "Tiquntha." Cureton (*Ancient Syriac Documents*, 161) comments: "This word has been so much distorted and disfigured by the transcribers that I am not able to recognise what is the place intended." Ramelli ("Possible Historical Traces," 71–72 n. 54) suggests it is to "Thiunta, a town North of Hierapolis, in Asia Minor, on the 'Persian road' from Edessa to the West, or, less probably, Thilaticomum, located in Osrhoene, South-East of Edessa, where the *ala septima Valeria praelectorum* stood."

F. *Artiqa*: according to Cureton (*Ancient Syriac Documents*, 161) this may

Gaius was guarding the districts around Caesar.[A] [3]Aristides then recounted before Tiberius the miracles Addai performed before King Abgar. [4]And when he had respite from war, he sent and killed some of the rulers of the Jews who were in Palestine.[B] [5]Hearing this, King Abgar rejoiced greatly that the Jews had received a fitting punishment.

The Organization of the Church of Edessa

77 [1]Many years after the apostle Addai built the church in Urhay and everything was acquired that was fitting for it and had made disciples of many from the city's inhabitants, he also built churches in the surrounding towns, both far and near. [2]He adorned and set them in order, appointed deacons and presbyters in them, taught those who would read the Scriptures in them, and taught the orders of the ministry within and without.[C] [3]After

---

refer to the city of Ortygia near Syracuse where Tiberius was known to have had a residence. Desreumaux (*Histoire*, 101 n. 161) corrects this confusion: "le texte confondrait cette île avec Capri, résidence habituelle de Tibère à partir de 26" ("the text confuses this island with Capri, the usual residence of Tiberius from 26"). Ramelli ("Possible Historical Traces," 71–72 n. 54) also suggests it could be a reference to "*Aricia/Aritia*, South-East of Rome, on the *Via Appia*" based on references from Tacitus, *Ann.* 6.32 and Josephus, *A.J.* 18.6.6.

A. *while Gaius was guarding the districts around Caesar*: the mention of Gaius along with Claudius and Tiberius suggests that the storyteller understood them to have ruled together in a manner similar to that of Diocletian's tetrarchy system. The storyteller's cultural memory only goes back as far as the existence of multiple rulers in the Roman Empire, confirming that *Doctr. Addai* cannot possibly date earlier than the fourth century when the co-rule of the empire had become normative.

B. Josephus, *A.J.* 18.4.3 mentions that Lucius Vitellius, appointed by Tiberius, removed Caiaphas from his position, though he does not mention that anyone was killed.

C. *the apostle Addai . . . within and without*: *Teach. Apos.* 6:9 states: "Edessa and all the countries around it on all its sides, Nisibis, Arabia, the whole North and the regions around it, and the South and the whole border regions (of) Mesopotamia received the apostolic hand of priesthood from the apostle Addai, one of the seventy-two apostles, who was teaching there, built a church, was the priest there and ministered in his capacity as the leader" (trans. Witakowski, *MNTA*). Both texts—which appear together in B—maintain the primacy of Edessa as the birthplace of Christianity in the region,

all of these things, he became ill with a sickness because of which he left this world. ⁴So he called Aggai before the whole assembly of the church and brought him near and made him leader and ruler[A] in his place. Palūt, who was a deacon, he made a presbyter, and 'Abšelama,[B] who was a scribe, he made a deacon.

The Testament of Addai

78 ¹While the nobles and chiefs were assembled and standing by him—Bar Kalbā,[C] Bar Zati,[D] Māryāhb son of Bar Šemeš,[E] Senaq bar 'Awidā,[F] and Peroz bar Patriq,[G] along with the rest of their fellows—the apostle Addai said to them:

---

from which all other towns received ordination.

A. *leader and ruler*: see the note in ch. 17 about these terms.

B. *Palūt . . . and 'Abšelama*: see the notes in ch. 68. The different figures move up in rank: Aggai's position is presumably just below a bishop; Palūt moves into the role of presbyter; 'Abšelama moves from scribe to deacon. This may reveal the early forms of the Edessene clergy at the time of *Doctr. Addai*'s final composition.

C. *Bar Kalbā*: see note in ch. 33.

D. *Bar Zati*: this name only appears here and must have been the name of a noble house in Edessa.

E. *Māryāhb son of Bar Šemeš*: it is unclear if this is the same Māryāhb as in ch. 1, who there is paired with Šemešgram. The name Bar Šemeš (lit. "Son of the sun") appears in one inscription and one mosaic, both dating to the third century (Drijvers, *Old-Syriac Inscriptions*, nos. 30 and 49; Segal, *Edessa*, pl. 43). More significantly, Māryāhb bar Šemeš is named in *Chron. Ed.* as a scribe of Edessa and one of the authors of the chronicle (Guidi, *Chronica Minora I*, 3). This may suggest that the storyteller knew of Māryāhb bar Šemeš as a figure of historical importance. His appearance in *Doctr. Addai* provides a great deal of verisimilitude and authority to the account.

F. *Senaq bar 'Awidā*: the name Bar Senaq appears in a third-century inscription (Drijvers, *Old-Syriac Inscriptions*, no. 63). It is unclear if this is the same 'Awidā as before. See the note in ch. 35 on his significance and his appearance again in ch. 66.

G. *Peroz bar Patriq*: on the name Peroz see the note in ch. 67. The name Patriq is from the Greek Πατρίκιος and the Latin *Patricius*. During the early Byzantine period it was not uncommon to see Greek and Latin names transferred into Semitic languages and vice versa.

[2]"You know and you[A] bear witness, all of you who hear me, that everything that I have preached to you and taught you, and (everything) you have heard from me, by these (teachings) I have conducted myself among you and you have even seen it in (my) actions. [3]Because the Lord thus commanded us that whatever we preach in words before people, we ourselves must perform in deed before all people. [4]According to the orders and laws which were set down[B] in Jerusalem, by which also my fellow apostles conducted themselves, so you also should not depart from them nor should you take anything away from them, even as I have conducted myself by them among you and have not turned from them, to the right or to the left, lest I become a foreigner to the promised salvation, which is being kept for those who conduct themselves according to these things.

cf. Matt 23:3; John 13:17

79 [1]"Therefore, watch over this ministry which you hold. [2]Stand in it with fear and trembling and serve every day. [3]Do not serve in it with vile habits, but with the excellence of faith. [4]Let the praises of Christ not cease from your mouth, and let not the laziness with regard to truth[C] of appointed times draw near to you. [5]Watch over the truth which you hold, the teaching of justice which you received, and the inheritance of life which I am entrusting to you. [6]For you will be compelled before the tribunal of Christ when he makes a reckoning with the shepherds and bishops and when he receives his money from the merchants with profitable interest. [7]For he is the Son of the King and he has gone to receive the kingdom, and he will return. And he will come and will make a resurrection for all humanity. [8]Then he will sit on the throne of justice and will judge the dead and the living, just as he told us.

cf. Matt 25:14–30// Luke 19:12–27

Matt 19:28//Luke 22:30

A. *you*: B lacks this second pronoun.

B. *set down*: B adds "for the disciples."

C. *laziness with regard to truth*: B has "in prayer" which probably makes more sense—that is, do not become weary in prayer. Phillips takes the reading in B as the primary one and Howard advocates for this as well. The word "in truth" (*bšrārā*) occurs only four words apart from another use of that word and is directly above it in manuscript A (separated by one line). It is possible that the scribe made an error due to parablepsis based on his copy of the text.

80 [1]"Let not the hidden eye of your mind be closed to the lofty height[A] lest your offences abound on the path on which there are no offences nor heinous wandering on its pathways. [2]Seek those who are lost, entreat those who stray, rejoice in those who are found, bind up those who are broken, and keep watch over those who are full. [3]For it is by your hands that Christ's sheep will be compelled. [4]Do not be concerned with passing honor. [5]For the shepherd who is concerned that he be honored by his flock, his flock is in worse standing than him. [6]Let your vigilance be great toward the innocent lambs whose angels behold the face of the invisible Father.

cf. Matt 18:10

81 [1]"Do not be a stumbling block to the blind;[B] rather, clear a path and a road in a rough place between the crucifying Jews and the erring pagans.[C] [2]With these two sides only[D] you do battle so that you might demonstrate the truth of the faith that you hold. [3]When you are silent, your modest, honorable appearance will engage in battle on your behalf, along with those who hate truth and love falsehood. [4]Do not mistreat the poor in front of the rich, for the harsh pain of their poverty is enough for them. [5]Do not be deceived by Satan's hateful designs,[E] lest you be stripped bare of the faith with which you are clothed,[F] for infidelity is easier than faith, just as sin is more readily done than righteousness.

cf. Mark 1:3 and par.

82 [1]"Therefore, watch out for the crucifiers and do not become their friends, lest you be liable[G] alongside those whose hands

---

A. *to the lofty height*: Syr. *men rumā 'elyā*. B has only "to the height." Philips translates as "by exalted pride." On the "eye of the mind" see the note in ch. 57.

B. *Do not be a stumbling block to the blind*: see above ch. 70.

C. *the crucifying Jews and the erring pagans*: the two primary enemies in *Doctr. Addai*.

D. *only*: lacking in B.

E. *Satan's hateful designs*: the figure of Satan is named here and in chs. 15 and 86. The Jews, erring pagans, and "those who hate truth and love falsehood" are undoubtedly included among those who have been deceived by "Satan's hateful designs," so the storyteller is once again creating a distinction between his community and others.

F. A lacuna in B begins here. The text resumes at ch. 92.

G. *watch out . . . be liable*: this is the third time in Addai's speech that this

are covered in the blood of Christ. [2]Know and bear witness that everything we are saying and teaching with regard to Christ is written in the book of the Prophets and was set down by them.[A] [3]Their words testify to our teaching about Christ's judgment, his suffering, his resurrection, and his ascension. [4]They do not realize that when they stand against us they are standing against the words of the prophets and that just as they persecuted the prophets in their lifetimes, so also now, after their deaths, they are persecuting the truth which is written in the Prophets.

cf. Matt 27:25

cf. Matt 5:12//Luke 6:23; Acts 7:52

83 [1]"Again: watch out for the pagans who worship the sun and the moon, Bel and Nebo, and the rest of those things which they call 'gods'[B]—though, by nature, they are not gods. [2]Avoid them, therefore, because they worship creatures and fabrications. Just as you heard before: all of that for which the Lord came to the world was that created things might not again be worshiped and honored,[C] because they exist at the beckoning of their Creator; [3]whenever he wishes he dismisses them and causes them to cease and they become as if they do not exist. [4]For the will that created

---

same formula has occurred with the term "watch out/over" (*'ezdahar*, the Ethpael of *zhar*) followed by the term "to be compelled/avenged/demanded" (*'ethtb'a*, the Ethpeal of *tb'a*). In the first two instances, it was a call to take care of the "sheep" (79:5–6; 80:2–3), whereas here it serves as a warning against collaborating with Jews. The positioning of Christians between "Jews" and "pagans" in this section suggests an environment of religious competition and antagonism, which would fit well the situation in Edessa between the time of Ephrem and the time of Rabbula.

A. *written in the book of the Prophets and was set down by them*: the appeal to the prophets has been a major theme in *Doctr. Addai* (see chs. 38, 40, 41). It is not surprising that the storyteller uses them as proofs for the understanding of Jesus and therefore advocates for their use in church (see ch. 68).

B. *worship . . . 'gods'*: see ch. 50 above. The warning here reinforces the idea that the differentiating between the storyteller's group and any other religious group is a primary feature of *Doctr. Addai*.

C. *Just as you heard before . . . be worshiped and honored*: see ch. 47, where the same phrase appears, but there the Lord came in order to announce to the world the resurrection. It may be that people in the storyteller's time were still participating in some cultic activities associated with different deities. In the 360s Ephrem was complaining that an annual "pagan" procession still took place between Edessa and Ḥārrān (see *Nis.* 33). Cultural habits die hard and it may be that although many people in Edessa had accepted Christianity, they continued to practice their habitual festivals.

the creatures has freed human beings from the bondage of the paganism of creatures. [5]For you know that, in the midst of their worship, death by the sword will find anyone who worships a king's servants along with the king.

84 [1]"Do not be too curious about secret matters[A] nor ask about hidden things which are written in the holy books you possess nor be judges of the words of the prophets—remember and see that they were spoken by the Spirit of God. [2]Whoever finds fault with the prophets finds fault with and casts judgment on the Spirit of God. [3]Far be you from this! [4]For the ways of the Lord are straight and the righteous walk on them without offense, but the infidels stumble on them because they do not have the hidden eye of the hidden mind, which has no need of investigations that have no profit except harm. [5]Remember the threatening judgment of the prophets—and the word of the Lord which determines their words—that the Lord judges by fire and all human beings will be examined by it.

cf. Heb 1:1

Hos 14:9

cf. 1 Pet 2:11

85 [1]"For this reason, like travelers and strangers, who board for the night and rise early to (go to) their homes, so you should regard yourselves in this world. [2]From now on, you are journeying to the places where the Son went in order to prepare (them) for all who are worthy of them. [3]The kings of countries, their hosts go before them and prepare a resting place in their honor. [4]But this king of ours, look: he has gone to prepare blessed mansions for his soldiers so that they may dwell in them.

cf. John 14:2–3

86 [1]"For God did not create human beings in vain, but so that they might worship and praise him, here and there forever. [2]Just as he does not pass away, so those who praise him shall not cease. [3]Therefore, regard with your eyes my death like a sleep in the

A. *too curious about secret matters*: this prohibition appears as a major theme in Ephrem's second *Metrical Discourse on Faith* (see Hayes, *Metrical Discourses*, 15–42). There is also a similar statement in *Hist. John*, which appears in A after *Doctr. Addai*. See Lollar, *History of John*, 190–91. It does not appear in a later manuscript tradition of *Hist. John* and so this warning about being too curious may be a theme in the St. Petersburg manuscript that the scribe/copyist wished to emphasize. The notion of not probing into or investigating matters too deeply reflects common fears of corruption in a religious context.

night, since I am bound and prostrate in its sickness. [4]Remember that by the Son's suffering, death, which governs human beings, has passed away and ceased. [5]Satan causes many to sin and battles with the faithful so that they might lack truth. [6]Like the cultivator who sets his hand on a ploughshare who cannot make straight furrows in front of him if he looks behind him, so you, who have been called to this gift of service, be careful lest you be troubled by the affairs of this world and be impeded from that to which you have been called.

cf. Luke 9:62

87 [1]"You shall love the rulers and judges who have been called to this faith, while showing them no favor.[A] [2]But if they stray, reprove them justly so that you might show the boldness of your uprightness and they might make amends, lest they again be governed by their own will. [3]Let this be your diligence all the days of your lives so that all of you might pursue beautiful things, while also counseling others about them. [4]For in these things people find their salvation before God.

cf. Jas 2:1

88 [1]"Now, read these books in the churches of Christ:[B] the Law and the Prophets and the Gospel, which you read each day before the people; the Letters of Paul, which Shemon Cephas sent from the city of Rome; and the Acts of the Twelve Apostles, which

---

A. *while showing them no favor*: Syr. *kad lā nāsbayn atūn bapehūn bm-edem*, lit. "while not being respecters of persons in anything."

B. *read these books in the churches of Christ*: compare this list to canon 10 in *Teach. Apos.* which names the Old Testament, the Prophets, and the "acts of the triumphs" of the apostles as the only appropriate books to be read in church. This same list is mentioned in *Pre. Pet. Rom.* Unfortunately, this portion of *Doctr. Addai* is missing from B, a manuscript in which *Teach. Apos.* and *Pre. Pet. Rom.* also appear with *Doctr. Addai*. The "Gospel" appears in the singular which could indicate the use of the *Diatessaron*, as mentioned in ch. 71. The idea of Peter sending the Epistles of Paul from Rome is unique to *Doctr. Addai*. No such thing is mentioned in the traditions of Peter and Paul in Syriac (i.e., *Pre. Pet. Rom.* and *Hist. Paul*). Nor is there mention of John the son of Zebedee with regard to the acts of the apostles. However, in *Hist. John*, John composes his Gospel after Matthew, Mark, and Luke (*Hist. John.* 32). This mention of the four-fold Gospels stands somewhat in tension in the manuscript between *Doctr. Addai* and *Hist. John*. Such tension may in fact reflect the situation of the fifth century in Edessa when, during the tenure of bishop Rabbula, the Edessene church transitioned from using the *Diatessaron* to using the four-fold Gospels.

John the son of Zebedee sent from Ephesus. ²Do not again read any others along with these, since there is no longer any other (book) in which is written the truth which you possess, except these books which you keep in that faith to which you have been called.ᴬ

89 ¹"Our lord King Abgar and his honorable nobles, who have heard all that I have spoken before you today, they are sufficient to be witnesses after my death that the Lord's instruction has been proclaimed carefully before all people and that I have not gained anything in this world by his word.ᴮ ²His word is sufficient for me, by which I have become rich and have caused many to become rich,ᶜ so that it may set me on the path on which I shall go, before Christ who sent for me. ³And I shall proceed on it to him.

cf. 2 Cor 8:9

90 ¹"For you know what I said to you, that the souls of all people who go forth from this body do not die, but they live and rise.ᴰ

A. *Do not read again . . . to which you have been called*: Rabbula, *Admon.* 10 states that "Books outside of the faith of the church may not be in the monasteries" (trans. from Phenix and Horn, *Rabbula Corpus*, 97). Rabbula's *Comm. Admon.* 43 states: "The priests and the deacons will ensure that the [book] of the separate Gospels (Syr. *ewangelyōn damparraše*) is in all the churches and that it is read." He continues in *Comm. Admon.* 44: "The priests must read the Gospel where there [are priests present] and there are no deacons present, and the priests must give the sign [i.e., the oil of blessing] if there are [priests present]" (trans. from Phenix and Horn, *Rabbula Corpus*, 113). In the context of *Doctr. Addai* this prohibition against reading "other" books appears confined to what is read in church. Otherwise one could wonder if the storyteller means his own story could not be read by anyone.

B. *Our lord King Abgar and his honorable nobles . . . by his word*: yet another direct reference to the Edessene nobility as the guarantors of the traditions of Addai. The backing of the nobility would have carried considerable social and economic capital. It is possible that the storyteller aligned himself with particular noble families in order to stand against other, competing sources of legitimacy, including the bishopric led by Rabbula.

C. *by which I have become rich and have caused many to become rich*: this statement stands in contrast to other places where Addai explicitly refuses to take any gifts or payment for his efforts at evangelizing Edessa. See chs. 13, 63, 93, and 97. Addai here maintains that his true gift and reward is the wealth brought by his teaching and evangelizing.

D. *For you know . . . they will live and rise*: Addai does not discuss resurrection explicitly in his teaching, but the theme is prominent in the narrative. In chs. 22–23 Protonike prays for her daughter to have life and that her soul

[2]They have mansions and a dwelling place of rest. [3]For the mind and intellect of the soul do not perish, because the eternal image of God is depicted in it. [4]For (the soul) is not like the body, which is without perception, so that it is unconscious of the hateful corruption which dwells within it. [5](The soul) is unable to receive the reward and recompense from without, since the labor did not belong to it alone, but also to the body in which it resided.[A]

91 [1]"Now, the rebels who do not know God, they repent without profit. [2]But you who belong to Christ, whose glorious name is set upon you and rules over you, he will direct you on the right path, so that you may proceed on it and arrive, and then proceed to that which is promised and kept for those who do not stray from it, and remain just as they were when called by Christ."

1 Cor 3:23

cf. Ps 23:3

cf. 1 John 2:25

cf. 1 Cor 7:21

92 [1]After the apostle Addai said this speech, he was silent and ceased. [2]Aggai, the maker of royal silks,[B] responded and he and Palūt and ʿAbšelāmā,[C] along with the rest of their fellows, said to the apostle Addai, [3]"Christ who sent you to us is a witness that

---

return to her body. See also chs. 58 and 87.

A. *For (the soul) . . . to the body in which it resided*: this discussion of sense perception, the soul, and its relationship to the body may be compared to Ephrem's ideas in his *Prose Refutations*. In *Hyp. 5*, Ephrem writes: "(The soul) is not able to do anything without (the body). For hearing enters into (the soul) through the ears; smell comes by (the body's) inhalation, by means of (the body's) eyes (the soul) sees images, with its mouth it examines tastes, with its heart it discerns knowledge, and with all of it every aspect, with the touch of its fingers it obtains a great and subtle sensation" (trans. from Possekel, *Evidence*, 193). Contrary to Ephrem, who believes that the heart is the conduit through which the soul receives knowledge, *Doctr. Addai* uses the terms *hawnā* and *madʿā* as properties belonging to the soul (*napšā*).

B. *Aggai, the maker of royal silks*: Desreumaux (*Histoire*, 110 n. 192) writes: "The clarification of Aggai's role with the king before his conversion may be a feature of the anti-Manichaean polemic: he who will become the Apostle's successor (see ch. 96) before Abgar is the real silk merchant, as opposed to Mani, who had that reputation" (trans. mine). Mani was said to have travelled to India and to Seleucia-Ctesiphon as a merchant who proclaimed his own message before Shapur I. In a similar way, Aggai is presented as a merchant of silks who, like Mani, will be the right hand of the king.

C. *ʿAbšelāmā*: this name appears in several narratives connected with the early Edessene church. A cemetery of the father of ʿAbšelāmā is mentioned in *Mart. Sharb.* and more precisely as the cemetery of ʿAbšelāmā son of Abgar in *Mart. Habib.*

you have taught us the true faith and have caused us to possess the true life. [4]Just as we have heard and received from you in the time that you were with us, thus we shall continue all the days of our lives. [5]We will flee from the worship of creatures and fabrications which our ancestors worshiped.[A] [6]We will not take part with the crucifying Jews.[B] [7]We will not abandon this inheritance which we have received from you but will go forth in it from this world.[C] [8]And just as you told us, on the day of the Lord, before the tribunal of the righteous judge, there he will return to us this inheritance."[D]

93 [1]After these things had been said, King Abgar stood and went to his palace along with all of his princes and nobles[E] of his kingdom, all of whom were grieving over (Addai), that he was dying. [2]Then (Abgar) sent to (Addai) clothes of honor and favor in which he might be buried.[F] [3]But when Addai saw them he sent word to him (saying), "In my life I took nothing from you.[G] [4]I will not defraud in myself the word of Christ who said to me, 'Do not take anything from any person and do not acquire anything in this world.'"[H]

A. *which our ancestors worshiped*: the promise to abandon "paganism" reinforces the polemic against Judaism and "paganism" throughout *Doctr. Addai*. See the example of Protonike in ch. 18 and similar admonitions from Addai in chs. 45 and 59. There are multiple mosaics from the region of Osrhoene containing portraits from classical myths, especially the *Iliad* and *Odyssey*, with Syriac inscriptions in them, indicating that classical Greek religious ideas were prominent in the region well into the third century. See Rigolio, "Syriac," 171–74.

B. B resumes here.

C. *We will not abandon this inheritance . . . from this world*: see ch. 79 where Addai mentions the inheritance of life which his gospel brings to the people of Edessa.

D. *Just as you told us . . . this inheritance*: see ch. 79.

E. *all of his princes and nobles*: B has only "his nobles."

F. *clothes of honor and favor in which he might be buried*: in a similar way, *Vit. Eph.* 42 describes Ephrem's refusal to be buried with any clothes or possessions.

G. *In my life I received nothing from you*: B adds, "and I will not now receive anything from you in my death."

H. *Do not take . . . this world*: this exact line appears nowhere in the Gospels. Desreumaux (*Histoire*, 111 n. 198) suggests that it could come from the

94 [1]Three days later, after these words were spoken by the apostle Addai and he had heard and received testimony of the teaching of his preaching from his ministers, he went forth from this world before all the nobles.[A] [2]It was the fifth day of the week, on the fourteenth of the month of Iyar.[B]

95 [1]There was great lamentation and bitter sorrow throughout the entire city. [2]And it was not Christians alone who were grieving over him, but even Jews and pagans who were in the city as well. [3]But King Abgar, more than anyone, was grieved over him—he and the princes of his kingdom. [4]In the sadness of his mind, he neglected and abandoned the honor of his kingdom on that day, weeping doleful tears for him along with everyone. [5]All the people of the city who saw him marveled at how much he suffered over him.

cf. John 11:36

96 [1]He bore him and buried him with great and exalted honor, like one of the princes when they die, and he set him in a great tomb with decorated sculptures[C]—the tomb in which were laid the house of 'Aryū,[D] the ancestors of King Abgar's fathers. [2]There

---

Diatessaron.

A. *before all the nobles*: the presence of the nobility at Addai's death is surely meant to establish the ties between the nobles of Edessa at the time of *Doctr. Addai*'s composition and the origins of Christianity in the city.

B. *fourteenth of the month of Iyar*: that is Thursday, May 14. The Anaphora (the liturgy performed on the feast days of particular saints) of Addai and Mār Māri, is still an important part of the liturgy of the Church of the East (see Mar Awa Royel, "Pearl of Great Price"). Addai's feast day does not appear in the regular Syrian Orthodox calendar.

C. *decorated sculptures*: lit. "sculptures of ornaments." A has *tsebthe* ("ornaments, embellishments, decorations") while B has *tseb'tā* ("fingers") which would indicate something like "sculptures of fingers," or perhaps "handmade sculptures." The traditional Anaphora of Addai (and Māri) has Addai buried in the church of Edessa that he helped establish. See Mar Awa Royel, "Pearl of Great Price."

D. *house of 'Aryū*: the purported founding dynasty of Urhay. The name is the Canaanite-Aramaic term for lion. This dynasty probably came into power around the 130s BCE. Segal (*Edessa*, 16–18) takes the burial of Addai in royal fashion as indicative of how the Edessene nobility would have been buried. If the tomb of the house of 'Aryū still existed in the fifth century, the storyteller is thus claiming that Addai's remains were still interred there. The next section says that the Christians would hold a yearly memorial, perhaps

he laid him sorrowfully, with sadness and great grief. [3]From time to time all the people of the church would go and pray there earnestly and each year would perform a memorial festival[A] in accordance with the command and instruction they had received from the apostle Addai and according to the word of Aggai, who was leader and ruler and his appointed successor to the See after him, by the hand of the priesthood which he received from him before everyone.

97 [1]Moreover, by that very hand (of the priesthood) which (Aggai) received from (Addai), he appointed priests and leaders in all this region of Mesopotamia.[B] [2]For they also held to his word, in the same manner as the apostle Addai himself, both hearing and receiving, as a good and faithful heir[C] of the apostle of the

---

similar to a saint's day celebration, but the way this is expressed suggests that such a ritual was not being performed by the Christians in the fifth century. This could indicate that one *raison d'être* of *Doctr. Addai* was to forge a more consistent and plausible connection between the Christians in the storyteller's time and the imagined past created in the narrative. The story effectively invents a myth of Christian origins of Edessa and simultaneously impresses upon the audience the need to observe "customs" that are prescribed in the story. We do not have any evidence that such customs were in fact observed at any point after the composition of *Doctr. Addai*, but the popularity of the story and Addai's character suggest that it is plausible.

A. *memorial festival*: Syr. *dūkrānā d'ūhdāne*. B has *dūkrānā d'ūndāne* "a festival of his departure." The term *dūkrānā* is used in reference to feast days of saints. See the comments on feast days in honor of Addai in the previous note. See also Desreumaux, *Histoire*, 112 n. 201.

B. *region of Mesopotamia*: this is somewhat in conflict with *Teach. Apos.* 6:9–10, which relates that Mesopotamia received the priesthood from Addai, while Persia, the lands of the Assyrians, Arameans, Medes and Babylon, the Huzites, Gilanians, Gog and Magog, and up to the borders of India all received ordination from Aggai. Later East Syriac traditions would omit Aggai and either trace their origins to Addai or, later, to Mār Māri.

C. *a good and faithful heir*: B has the plural "good and faithful heirs." The difference here is between Aggai or his successors. The context supports both interpretations. The text of A suggests an attempt to recognize the legitimacy of Aggai as the direct heir of Addai. The text of B stresses the legitimacy of all the successors of Addai, including, in this context, all the bishops in Mesopotamia. The storytellers behind the *Acts of Mār Māri* use this legitimacy to support the authority of the traditions about Mār Māri in Mesopotamia.

divine Christ. [3]He[A] took neither silver nor gold from any person, nor did gifts of princes come near to him. [4]For instead of gold and silver, he enriched the church of Christ with the souls of the faithful.[B]

cf. Matt 10:9

The Successors of Addai

98 [1]The whole *qyāmā* of men and women[C] were chaste and honorable, holy and pure, living undefiled in solitude[D] and modesty, honorably in diligent service, relieving the burden of the poor and by their visitations to the sick. [2]For their ways were full of praise from those who saw, and their customs were clothed in honor by strangers, so that even the priests of the temple of Nebo

A. *He*: this appears to refer to Aggai in the context, but grammatically it is ambiguous. Desreumaux inserts Aggai's name here.

B. *he enriched the church of Christ with the souls of the faithful*: see the note in ch. 89.

C. *qyāmā of men and women*: probably a reference to the famous *bnay/bartā qyāmā* (sons/daughters of the covenant). This group has been studied quite extensively as a formative aspect of Syrian monasticism. The major fourth-century Syriac writers Ephrem and Aphrahat write about these individuals who seem to have held a place of prominence in the Syrian church from a very early date. They probably served in special capacities in the rituals of the church and, as this passage clarifies, they were probably celibate and lived as "single" people (see the next note on the special term *iḥidāyā*). These men and women aimed at imitating the life of Christ in extreme ways, particularly in the giving up of property and the devotion to celibacy. There is little reason to doubt that the storyteller of *Doctr. Addai* and his readers would have known this group. The term *qyāmā* is tricky to translate (see Griffith, "Asceticism in the Church of Syria"), so I have simply left it untranslated. Cureton translates it as "the whole state of the men and women"; Philips mistranslates it as "all the chiefs of the men and women"; Desreumaux is closer to the Syriac with "l'Ordre"; Illert has "der ganze Bund der Männer und Frauen." On the *qyāmā*, see especially the works of Robert Murray ("'Circumcision of the Heart'"; and *Symbols*).

D. *solitude*: Syr. *iḥidāyith*. This term is distinctly connected with the *qyāmā* mentioned in the previous note. The term may be traced back to the early translations of John 1:18, which refer to Christ as the "one and only God" (*iḥidāyā alāhā*). The *iḥidāye* were those elite members of the *qyāmā* who practiced a strict imitation of Christ. Their "singleness" was marked by their celibacy, but also by their station and role in the liturgy. See Brock, *Luminous Eye*, 131–41.

and Bel constantly divided honor with them in their honorable appearance, in the truth of their words, in the boldness they possessed, and in the freedom which was unbound from avarice and was above reproach.[A]

99 [1]Whenever anyone saw them, they would run to meet them[B] so that they might inquire honorably after their welfare, because even their appearance spread peace upon those who saw (them). [2]Their words of peace spread in the form of nets over rebels as they enter into the midst of the fold of justice and truth. [3]There was not one person who saw them and was ashamed of them, because they did nothing that was unjust or unsuitable. [4]For these reasons, they displayed unveiled faces in the preaching of their instruction to all people. [5]For that which they said to others and advised they displayed by their deeds in their own persons,[C] and those pupils who saw that their deeds accompanied their words, many became their disciples without persuasion and confessed in Christ the King, while praising the God who turned them to him.

A. *above reproach*: lit. "not held under accusation." This description of *qyāmā* of the imagined past may be a critique leveled at the ascetics of the storyteller's time. The *Comm. Admon.* of Rabbula give the impression that from the bishop's perspective, asceticism in the region of Edessa was somewhat disorderly and in need of reforms. The storyteller of *Doctr. Addai* may have shared such an outlook of the monks in the area. The storyteller's solution to this was to compare the monks of his day with the monks of an imagined, ideal past in which the "true" monks followed the example of the founder of Edessa's Christianity: Addai.

B. *Whenever anyone saw them, they would run to meet them*: B has "There was no one who saw them who did not run to meet them."

C. *in their own persons*: B has the singular: "in their own person."

100 [1]Some years after the death of King Abgar, one of his rebellious sons[A] who was disobedient to the truth[B] rose to power. [2]He sent word to Aggai, who was presiding over the church: "Make gold tiaras for me as you did for my ancestors before." [3]Aggai sent in reply: "I will not abandon the ministry of Christ, which was entrusted to me by Christ's disciple, and make evil tiaras."[C] [4]When (the king) saw that he was not obedient to him, he went and broke his legs while he was sitting in the church giving a homily.[D]

A. *one of his rebellious sons*: only one son of Abgar is named in *Doctr. Addai* (ch. 63). According to *Chron. Zuq.* 97–98 "Ma'nu son of Abgar, king of Edessa, died, and his brother Ma'nu reigned for fourteen years" (trans. Harrak, *Chronicle of Zuqnīn*, 162). The use of the family names of the Abgarids leads to obvious confusion. The chronology could work if we take Abgar Ukkāmā as the king of Edessa in the narrative (see the note in ch. 63). It could also work, however, for Abgar VIII the Great, whose father was Ma'nu and who had at least two sons: Abgar Severus and, according to *Chron. Ed.*, Ma'nu, who "reigned" in Edessa from 214–240 CE. This Ma'nu was likely only a king in name, since Edessa had officially become a *colonia* by 214. If, as many have suggested, the Abgar in *Doctr. Addai* represents Abgar the Great, his son Ma'nu in ch. 63 was evidently accepted by the storyteller as a Christian king, like his father. The other, "rebellious" son would have to have been Abgar Severus, who was arrested by Emperor Caracalla, after being invited to Rome, under the pretext of mistreating the citizens of Edessa (Cassius Dio, *Hist.* 78.12.1; see Segal, *Edessa*, 14; and Ross, *Roman Edessa*, 57–64). Moreover, Cassius Dio accuses: "Abgarus, king of Osrhoeni, when he had once got control of the kindred tribes, visited upon their leaders all the worst forms of cruelty. Nominally he was compelling them to change to Roman customs, but in fact he was indulging his authority over them to the full" (*Hist.* 78.12.1). This kind of treatment would appear to coincide with what *Doctr. Addai* says about Abgar's successor.

B. *to the truth*: B has "peace" instead of "truth."

C. *evil tiaras*: B has the singular.

D. *giving a homily*: every modern editor to date has taken this verb as *mtargem*, an active participle from *targem*. It could also, however, be the Ethp'el/Ethpa'al participle of *rgam*, "to be stoned/subject to stoning." On the one hand, *targem* fits the context of Aggai sitting in the church at the time. On the other hand, the next clause begins, "As he was dying . . ." meaning that whatever was done to him led to his death. If we take the term as a participle of *targem*, then we must conclude that the breaking of his legs caused Aggai's death. If we take it as a participle of *rgam*, then we have another, more plausible cause of death. If it is the latter case, then this clause would read something like, "he went and broke his legs while he was sitting in the church and he was stoned/subjected to stoning." The reference to the breaking of his

101 [1]As he was dying, he directed Palūt and ʿAbšelāmā: "Place me and bury me in this house in whose name[A] I now die." [2]So, just as he had directed them, they placed him within the middle entryway of the church, between the men and women.[B] [3]There was great and bitter sorrow in the whole church and the whole city, similar to the suffering of sorrow which had happened when the apostle Addai died.

102 [1]Now, because with the breaking of his legs (Aggai) died quickly and rapidly, he was not able to lay his hand on Palūt. [2]Palūt then went to Antioch and received the hand of the priesthood from Serapion the bishop of Antioch.[C] [3]And Bishop Serapion of Antioch himself had received the hand (of the priesthood) from Zephyrinus,[D] bishop of Antioch,[E] from the succession of the hand of the priesthood of Shemon Cephas, who himself had received it from the Lord, and was bishop there in Rome for twenty-five years in the days of Caesar who had reigned there for thirteen years.[F]

---

legs in 102:1 highly suggests that *mtargem* is the preferred reading.

A. *in whose name*: B has "in whose truth."

B. *between the men and women*: the separation of men and women during worship was a common practice in the fourth and fifth centuries in both Christian churches and synagogues.

C. *received . . . Serapion the bishop of Antioch*: as Desreumaux points out, the mention of Antioch conferring authority on Palūt legitimizes the church of Edessa under the see of Antioch. By then linking Antioch's authority to Rome, Edessa may be seen as in perfect unity with the larger Western church. Forging such a link in the narrative would no doubt have made sense in the context of Rabbula's tenure as bishop—whether *Doctr. Addai* was supporting his regime or opposing it. In terms of time frame, the two bishops hardly add up, though they do align with the rule of Abgar VIII the Great like so many other events and characters in the narrative. Serapion was bishop starting in 189 or possibly 192 CE, whereas Zephyrinus's tenure at Rome began in 202, so Serapion could not have received ordination and authority from Zephyrinus. Ross (*Roman Edessa*, 135) rightly summarizes: "All these connections give the community that traced its religious ancestry to Palūt a double claim to authority: as the inheritor of Jesus' blessing via Addai and Aggai, and as the duly appointed arm of the Church of Rome."

D. *Zephyrinus*: bishop of Rome beginning in 202 CE. He could not have ordained Serapion, since Zephyrinus became bishop later. See the note above.

E. *Antioch*: this is an error and is indeed changed in B to "Rome."

F. *Shemon Cephas . . . thirteen years*: thus Palūt is able to trace his own

103 [1]As is the custom in the kingdom of King Abgar and in all kingdoms,[A] everything that is spoken before him is recorded and placed in the archives.[B] [2]Thus, Lebubnā[C] bar Senaq, bar 'Abšadar, the king's scribe, recorded these things about the apostle Addai, from beginning to end, while Ḥanan, the king's faithful archivist, set his hand as a witness and placed it in the archives of the royal books, in which the statutes and laws are placed. [3]Records of things bought and sold are also kept there securely and without any form of negligence.

The Doctrine of Addai the Apostle is completed.

---

apostolic authority, and that of the Church of Edessa, back to Peter. That Peter was bishop for 25 years is also maintained by *Hist. Sim. Ceph.* 33 and *Pre. Pet. Rom.* 10:7. See Eastman, *Many Deaths*, 93–102 on resolving the issues of dating Peter's death in these sources.

A. *in all kingdoms*: here B adds "that everything that the king orders."

B. *archives*: lit. "among the records." The appeal to the archives is likely a move by the storyteller to add credibility and authority to his story. Eusebius mentions the archives of Edessa and several later chronicles mention Edessa's civic archives. They also play a role in other texts in B, including *Mart. Sharb*. This may be an editorial feature by scribes to add to the verisimilitude of their stories and create a sense of credibility. See Debié, "Record Keeping."

C. *Lebubnā*: also mentioned in ch. 35. His figuring into the story as the "faithful archivist" and the storyteller creates a historical air around the fiction. Camplani ("Traditions," 258) writes: "perhaps we are dealing here with a propagandistic leitmotiv rather than with a true derivation from archives. Already present within the text of [Eusebius's version], this would then have been further emphasized by the [*Doctrine of Addai*], in order to confer greater authority upon the story. It is a leitmotiv that Eusebius would have reproduced for reasons that are patently apologetic in nature."

2

Appendix A

The Development of the Abgar/Jesus Correspondence

1. Eusebius, *Ecclesiastical History* 1.13.1–22

Eusebius of Caesarea is the first to mention the correspondence between Abgar and Jesus. There is reason to believe that the correspondence predates Eusebius, but official record of the legend begins with the church historian in the first half of the fourth century.[1] Eusebius names Thaddaeus as the apostle sent to Edessa. It is noteworthy, however, that he also says that it is Judas Thomas who commissions Thaddaeus, a role that is maintained in subsequent iterations of the story, including *Doctr. Addai*. In 384 CE, Egeria visited Edessa with the expressed interest of visiting the shrine of Thomas. The fifth-century Armenian tradition goes so far as to establish Thomas as the brother of Thaddaeus, such that Thomas continues to play a significant role in the myths of Edessa's Christianization.[2]

Eusebius's version of the correspondence is typically considered the earliest extant form. This preeminent status has been somewhat challenged

1. On the pre-history of the legend, see Palmer, "King Abgar."

2. Palmer ("King Abgar," 29) posits an early version of the legend in which Judas Thomas is the missionary sent to Edessa.

by suggestions of an earlier form found in the Oxford/Cairo papyri,[3] and by linguistic analyses indicating that Eusebius relied on a Syriac original.[4] The translation here is based on the Greek edition of Eusebius produced by Eduard Schwartz.[5]

[1]The manner of the story of Thaddaeus unfolded as follows:

Since the divinity of our Lord and Savior Jesus Christ became notorious among all people because of his wonderworking power, myriads were led to him, even those from the most remote places from Judea, in hopes of healing from diseases and sufferings of all kinds. [2]In this way, Abgar, the reputable ruler of the peoples beyond the Euphrates, who was perishing in his body from terrible and incurable suffering of a kind beyond human ability to heal, when he learned much, both of the name of Jesus and of the miracles witnessed unanimously by all, he became his suppliant and sent to him via a letter-carrier, praying to gain deliverance from his disease.

[3]Now at that time, he (Jesus) did not give heed to his summoning, but granted him a letter of his own, promising to send one of his disciples for the healing of his disease as well as for his salvation and that of all his relations. [4]The terms of his promise to him were, indeed, not far off in their fulfillment. After his resurrection from the dead and his return to heaven, Thomas, one of the twelve apostles, by divine influence sent out Thaddaeus, himself elected from among the number of the seventy of Christ's disciples, to Edessa as herald and evangelist of the teaching about Christ, and through him all the terms of the promise of our Savior received satisfaction. [5]We possess also documentary evidence of these events, which were taken from the archives at Edessa, which was at the capital city. Indeed, in the public records there, which contain what was accomplished in past times by Abgar, these events also may be found preserved from that time until now. But there is nothing equal to hearing the letters themselves, which were extracted from the archives[6] by us. What is said in them, when translated from the Syrian language, is as follows:

3. See below the hypothesis of Peppermüller, "Griechische Papyrusfragmente."

4. Polański, "Translation, Amplification, Paraphrase."

5. My thanks to my graduate assistant Matthew San Miguel for his painstaking work of comparing the Eusebian text to all other Greek versions, and for his helpful suggestions regarding English translation.

6. *the archives*: in *Doctr. Addai* the narrator claims that the story was held in the archives of Edessa. Even if this is a fictional account, the reference to the archives suggests their authority and thereby this mention of civic archives is intentional as a mark of

A copy of the letter written by Abgar the Toparch to Jesus and sent to him in Jerusalem through Ananias the courier.

[6]Abgar Ouchama, the Toparch, to Jesus the Good Savior who has appeared in the region of Jerusalem: greeting. The matters about you and about your healings have reached my ear—how they are accomplished by you without medicines or herbs. For, so they say, you make the blind see, the lame walk; you cleanse lepers, and cast out unclean spirits and demons; you heal those who suffer from long-term ailments, and you even raise the dead. [7]And when I heard all these things about you, I determined in my mind that you must be one of two things: either you are God and having descended from heaven, you perform these feats, or you are a Son of God who does such things. [8]For this reason, therefore, I am writing to implore you to make haste to me and to heal the suffering which I have. I have also heard that the Jews mock you and plan to do you harm. I have a quite small but majestic city which is satisfactory for both of us.

[9]*The reply of Jesus to Abgar, the Toparch, through Ananias the courier.*

[10]Blessed are you who believes in me not having seen me. For it is written about me that those who have seen me will not believe in me and that those who have not seen me shall believe and will live.[7] Now, about what you wrote to me, that I come to you: it is necessary for me to fulfill everything for which I was sent here and after thus fulfilling it, to be taken up to the one who sent me. When I have been taken up, I will send to you one of my disciples so that he might heal your suffering and bring life to you and those who are with you.

[11]To these letters these further events are appended in the Syrian language:

After Jesus was taken up, Judas, who is also Thomas, sent the apostle Thaddaeus, one of the seventy, who came and stayed with Tobias son of Tobias. When news was heard about him, it was reported to Abgar: "An apostle of Jesus has come here, just as he wrote to you." [12]Then, Thaddaeus began to heal every disease and weakness by the power of God so that everyone was amazed. Now, when Abgar heard the great and marvelous feats he performed, and how he was healing, he had it in mind that he was the one about whom Jesus wrote saying, "When I have been taken up, I will send to

---

authenticity. See Debié, "Record Keeping," 410.

7. Quoting John 20:29.

you one of my disciples who will heal your suffering."[8] [13]Then, having summoned Tobias with whom (Thaddaeus) resided, he said, "I have heard that a certain man of power has come and has been staying in your house. Bring him to me." So Tobias, coming to Thaddaeus, said to him, "The Toparch Abgar summoned me and told me to bring you to him so that you may heal him." Thaddaeus said, "I will go up since I have been sent to him by means of a miracle."

[14]So, Tobias, having risen early on the next day, came to Abgar, bringing Thaddaeus with him. Now, as Thaddaeus entered, Abgar's magistrates were present and standing around, (and) immediately at his entrance, a great vision appeared to Abgar in the face of the apostle Thaddaeus. When Abgar saw this, he knelt before Thaddaeus and wonder captivated all who were present; for they had not seen the vision, which had appeared to Abgar alone.

[15]He asked Thaddaeus, "Truly, are you a disciple of Jesus the Son of God, who told me, 'I will send to you one of my disciples who will heal you and give you life'"?[9] Thaddaeus replied, "Since you have believed greatly in the one who sent me, for this reason I was sent to you. Again: if you should believe in him, the requests of your heart shall be granted in proportion to your belief."

[16]Abgar said to him, "So much have I believed in him, that I wished to muster a force to obliterate the Jews who crucified him, but I was prevented from this by the Roman Empire." Thaddaeus said, "Our Lord has fulfilled the will of his Father and after fulfilling it he was taken up to the Father." [17]Abgar said, "I also have believed in him and in his Father." Thaddaeus replied, "For this reason, I set my hand upon you in his name." As soon as he did this, immediately he was healed of the disease and suffering which he had.

[18]And Abgar marveled how just as he had heard about Jesus, so in fact he had received through his disciple Thaddaeus, who healed him without medicines or plants; and not him alone, but also Abdu son of Abdu, who had gout. He also came and fell at his feet and, receiving prayers through his hand, he was healed. And many others of their fellow citizens he healed,

---

8. *who will heal your suffering*: a slight grammatical variation appears between this statement and the one from the letter. The letter contains a purpose clause in the subjunctive whereas this statement has a relative clause in the indicative.

9. *who will heal you and give you life*: a further grammatical variation on this statement, which has been repeated a second time.

performing great marvels and preaching the message[10] of God. [19]After these things, Abgar said, "You, Thaddaeus, do these things by the power of God and we have marveled at them. But beyond these miracles, I pray you to explain to me about the coming of Jesus, how it happened, and about his power and by what sort of power he performed these feats of the kind that I have heard."

[20]Thaddaeus replied, "For now, I will be silent. But since I was sent to proclaim the message, tomorrow, gather your entire city to me and I will proclaim over them and sow in them the message of life, both about the coming of Jesus, just how it happened, and about his mission, for what reason he was sent by the Father; as well as about his power and his deeds and the mysteries which he spoke in the world; as well as by what sort of power he performed these feats, and about his new preaching, and his lowliness and humiliation; and how he humbled himself and put off and minimized his divinity and was crucified, descended into Hades, and tore apart the division which had not ever been torn apart; and he raised the dead and descended alone, but ascended with a great multitude to his Father."[11] [21]Therefore, Abgar commanded his citizens to come together in the morning to hear the preaching of Thaddaeus. And after this, he ordered the gold and silver be given to him, but (Thaddaeus) did not receive it saying, "If we have left behind our own possessions, how can we receive the possessions of others?"

[22]These events took place in the 340th year.[12] Here I will leave for the time being this useful note, translated literally from the language of the Syrians.

10. *message*: Grk. λόγος.

11. Some Eusebius manuscripts add, "And how he is seated at the right hand of God the Father with glory in heaven, and how he will come again with power to judge the living and the dead."

12. *the 340th year*: Eusebius records here a date according to the Seleucid calendar, which Syriac Christians used well into the Middle Ages (see Debié, "Syriac Historiography"). The Seleucid era began in 311/312, which would mean this date corresponds to 29/30 CE. The retainment of this dating system by Eusebius is a significant verisimilitude. It suggests that he may be telling the truth that this was in fact a translation from Syriac. In his descriptive analysis of the Greek and Syriac texts of the letters, Polański ("Translation, Amplification, Paraphrase," 172) concludes that "Eusebius' version of Abgar's *Letter* is a translation from Syriac."

2. Egeria, *Itinerarium* 19.5–19

Egeria's witness to the Abgar/Jesus correspondence and its development should not be underestimated. Thanks to the work of Paul Devos, we know that Egeria was in Edessa in the year 384 CE.[13] Thus, we may say with confidence that the contents of the letters developed within the span of some fifty years between Eusebius's publication of them and Egeria's hearing them read aloud at the gates of Edessa. Not only do we find the addition of the promise of divine protection, but Egeria herself admits that the version read to her in Edessa "is in fact longer" than the version she knew at her home (probably in Spain). Egeria's travelogue survives in only one manuscript and is missing much of the beginning of her travels. It dates to the eleventh century and is notoriously difficult to decipher in places.[14] The following translation draws from the Latin edition by Wilkinson and the translation by McGowan and Bradshaw.

[5]The holy bishop of (Edessa) was a very devout man, both monk and confessor, who welcomed me and said to me, "I can see, daughter, that your great faith has brought you on so great a journey that you have come to this place from the other end of the world. So, if you please, let us show you what are all the places Christians should visit here." I first gave thanks to God and then eagerly entreated him that we might condescend to what he offered.

[6]He then led me first to the palace of King Abgar and there he showed me an enormous portrait of him—of great likeness, so they said—made of marble which shone greatly as if it was made of pearl. Without a doubt, the countenance of Abgar showed that this was a wise and honorable man. Then the holy bishop told me, "That is King Abgar. Before he saw the Lord he believed in him, that he was truly the Son of God." There was also next to this portrait a similar one made of the same marble, which he told me was Abgar's son Magnus, who similarly had a charming countenance.

[7]We then went inside the palace where there were pools full of fish, the likes of which I had never beheld—so great, so colorful, and they tasted so good. At present, the city has no other water in its interior but this, which flows from the palace and is like a massive river of silver. [8]Then the holy bishop told me the following story about this water:

13. Devos, "La date du voyage."

14. Wilkinson, *Egeria's Travels*; and McGowan and Bradshaw, *Pilgrimage of Egeria*. My thanks to Brandon W. Hawk for his many helpful suggestions on my translation.

"After King Abgar wrote a letter to the Lord and the Lord wrote back[15] through Ananias the courier, just as it is written in the letter, the Persians, at a much later time, came down upon us and surrounded the city. [9]Immediately Abgar took the Lord's letter with his whole army to the gate and prayed aloud and said, 'Lord Jesus, you promised us that no enemies would enter this city; see, now, how the Persians attack us!' After saying this, the king held up the letter openly in his upraised hand, and suddenly, outside the city, so great a darkness fell over the eyes of the Persians, who had already come three miles outside the city, and the darkness was so confusing to them that they could scarcely set up camp and patrol even three miles outside of the city.

[10]"So confused were the Persians that they were unable to see where they might enter the city, so they besieged the city, which was now surrounded by enemies all around, and although they were three miles away, they nevertheless besieged it for a few months. [11]Then, since they saw no possible way to enter the city, they determined to kill those who were in the city by thirst. Now, at that time, my daughter, that mountain which you see above the city administered the water to the city. As soon as the Persians realized this, they diverted the water from the city and made a watercourse away from the city to where they had set up their camp. [12]On that day, in that very moment when the Persians diverted the water, God commanded these fonts which you see in this place to spring forth at once; since that day until now these fonts continue flowing by the grace of God. But that water which the Persians had diverted also dried up at that same time, so that they who were besieging the city did not have anything to drink for even one day. And this is apparent even until today, for since then there has not appeared any moisture (in the watercourse). [13]Thus, by God's will, just as he had promised, they were forced to go home, which is in Persus. And afterwards, if ever enemies determined to come and besiege this city, this letter is produced and is read at the gate and immediately, by God's will, all enemies are driven away."

[14]The holy bishop then related that, "Where the fonts had sprung forth was beforehand inside the city and below Abgar's palace. Abgar's palace was

---

15. *wrote back*: Lat. *rescripserat*. This implies that Jesus responded with his own letter, but Wilkinson (*Egeria's Travels*, 116) translates the verb as "sent his answer," which could mean a verbal response to Ananias. Illert (*Doctrina Addai*, 127) represents the Latin better: "nachdem König Abgar an den Herrn geschrieben und der Herr dem Abgar durch den Schnelläufer Ananias schriftlich Antwort gegeben hatte" ("after King Abgar wrote to the Lord and the Lord answered Abgar in writing through the courier Ananias").

on a slightly higher ground, as is apparent today, you see. For at that time there was a custom that whenever palaces were built, it was always on high ground. [15]But after these fonts sprung forth in this place, then Abgar made this palace here for his son Magnus, who is the one whose portrait you saw placed next to his father, so that these fonts are enclosed within the palace."

[16]After the holy bishop had related all of this, he said to me, "Let us go now to the gate through which the courier Ananias came in with that letter I mentioned." Then, when we came to that gate the bishop stopped, said a prayer, and read the letters themselves to us and blessed us saying another prayer. [17]Then the holy man reported to us saying that from that day when the courier Ananias came into the gate with the Lord's letter until this day, it has been observed that no one who is unclean or mourning has passed through the gate, nor has any corpse been taken out through the gate. [18]The holy bishop then showed us Abgar's memorial: an immense tomb for his entire family, very beautiful, although built in an old style. Then he led us also to the upper palace, which Abgar had first possessed, and then showed us other desirable things that were there.

[19]It also gave me great joy that I received from the holy man the letters of Abgar to the Lord and of the Lord to Abgar, which the holy bishop had read to us. While I have copies at home, it gave me great joy that I received them here from him also, since perhaps a lesser version has come to our home, because what I received here is in fact longer. If our Lord Jesus allows and I return home, you shall read it, my dear ladies.

3. Inscriptions

3.1 Alkat-Hadji-Kevi (Pontus)

While excavating in Alkat-Hadji-Kevi, near modern Amasaya, Turkey, Franz Cumont found a fourth-century inscription on a fountain that contains the Abgar/Jesus correspondence. Cumont provides a complete copy of the inscription, which itself is very fragmentary.[16] To fill in the lacunae, Cumont used other versions of the correspondence, including another inscription found by J. G. C. Anderson in Çorum (see no. 3.3 below). This inscription is significantly early, probably even predating the final form of *Doctr. Addai*. Importantly, it appears to include the promise of divine protection, which is not included in Eusebius's version, but was known in

---

16. Cumont, "Nouvelles inscriptions," esp. 326.

Edessa as early as 384 CE when Egeria visited the city. The promise of protection was an obviously attractive feature of the correspondence. While some evidence demonstrates that the Abgar/Jesus correspondence was used for apotropaic purposes, inscriptions like this one appear to have been intended to ward off enemies from attacking cities. In fact, bishop Eulogius of Edessa told Egeria this very thing.

I have provided here a translation of Cumont's reconstructed Greek text. Line divisions, here and in the translations of the other inscriptions and papyri, preserve the divisions in the original sources. The word fragments in italics are transliterated letters of words that cannot be confidently reconstructed. The reader should note that text appearing inside the brackets "[ ]" represents Cumont's reconstruction and everything outside of the brackets is found on the surviving inscription.[17]

[The Savior's reply]
[Because those who have seen me] do not believe in m[e, so that those who have not
seen me might believe and live. Now, about what you wrote to me
to come to you: it is necessary that I ful]f[ill everything for] which I was sent here
[and after thus fulfilling it, to be taken up to the one who sent me.
And when I have been taken up, I will send you one of] my disciples who will he
[al your] s[uffering and eternal life . . . will give to you and to your city
so that none of your enemies should gain] c[on]trol [over it ...]

3.2 Edessa

In 1914, two German researchers published a Greek inscription from Edessa, located just west of the citadel in the area known as the "Forty Caverns/Tombs."[18] The inscription contains the reply of Jesus to Abgar in eleven lines of text. This version of the reply of Jesus is notable for a few reasons. First, as in the Alkat-Hadji-Kevi inscription, it contains the promise of protection for the city, once again showing that this promise became a standard part of the *textus receptus* of the correspondence at an early stage in its

17. The reconstructed text with a German translation may be found in Illert, *Doctrina Addai*, 178–79.

18. See Nau, "Une inscription grecque d'Édesse."

development. Second, and more strikingly, the Edessa inscription conflates the figures of Thaddaeus (!) and Thomas, suggesting that they are the same person. The collapsing of the two apostolic figures is likely an attempt at solving the dilemma created by multiple versions of the story: who, exactly, came to Edessa? Andrew Palmer has suggested that the earliest (oral?) layer of the story probably claimed that Judas Thomas himself came to Edessa, as this appears to be what Egeria thought. Eusebius then records a tradition where Thomas merely sent another apostle, Thaddaeus. The local Edessene version (*Doctr. Addai*) then altered this name in order to draw explicit comparisons with the Manichaeans in the city. This inscription thus sought to bring clarity to the situation by identifying Thomas as Thaddaeus.[19]

Based primarily on the conflation of the two apostles, the original editors of the inscription dated it after the composition of the *Acts of Thaddaeus* (ca. 550 CE). Palmer argues that *Acts Thad.* actually originated in Syriac, in Edessa, and was adapted from *Doctr. Addai*.[20] The inscription in the "Forty Caverns" at least demonstrates knowledge of the Thaddaeus tradition in Edessa by the sixth century. Given the increasing popularity of the story of the image of Christ by this period and its connections with the Abgar/Jesus correspondence and the city of Edessa, it is thus conceivable that someone would attempt to sort out the conflicting accounts about the apostles vis-à-vis Edessa's conversion myth. The translation is based on Nau's text.[21]

Blessed are you, Abgar, and your city, which is called Edessa! Blessed are you because you believed in me, not having seen me, and because health will be prepared for you in everything.

Now, about what you wrote to me, that I come to you: it is necessary to fulfill that for which I was sent here and after fulfilling (it) to be taken up to the Father who sent me.

But I will send to you one of my disciples named Thaddaeus, who is also Thomas, who also will heal your suffering and bring both eternal life and peace to you and to all those with you. And for your city, he will do what is necessary so that none of your enemies shall prevail over it until the end of the world. Amen. The Letter of our Lord Jesus Christ.

19. See Drijvers, "Facts and Problems"; and Drijvers, "Addai und Mani." The connection between Thaddaeus and Thomas is also made by the Armenian translation, dated as early as the fifth century.

20. See Palmer, "*Logos* of the Mandylion," 146.

21. Also reproduced in Illert, *Doctrina Addai*, 180–81.

3.3 Gurdja (Çorum)

J. G. C. Anderson published this almost complete inscription in 1900.[22] It was found on the wall of a mosque in the village of Gurdja, a few miles west of the city of Çorum, Turkey. He dated the inscription to the fourth century: "the letters are distinctly 'Byzantine' in character, while the small, rectangular lettering of the Tchorum stone is better than that of most fourth century."[23] Aside from the inclusion of the divine protection promise, the inscription is quite close to Eusebius's version of the letters. As Anderson notes, it shares some interesting resemblances with the door frame inscription from Ephesus (see no. 3.5 below). Like the Alkat-Hadji-Kevi (no. 3.1 above) and Edessa (no. 3.2 above) inscriptions, this one was probably inscribed as a means of protection against invasion, with the power of Jesus' words perceived as effective in keeping safe any city that inscribes the words on their gates. The translation comes from the transcription provided by Anderson. The Greek text and German translation may be found in Illert's volume.[24]

The letter of Abgar to God the Savior:
Abgar Ouchama the toparch to Jesus the Good Savior who appeared in the city of Jerusalem, greet[ing].
The matters about you and of your healings have reached my ear, how without medicines or herbs | they are accomplished by you. So, they say you make the blind to see, the lame to walk; | you cleanse lepers and cast out unclean spirits and demons; and those | who suffer from lo[n]g-term ailments you h[e]a[l], and you even raise the dead. And when | I heard all these things about you, I determined in my mind that you must be one of two things: either | you are God and having descended [f]rom heaven you perform these feats, or you are a Son | of God who does such things. Fo[r th]is reason, having written, I implore you to make haste | to me and to [he]al the suffering which [I have]. For I have also heard that the Jews | mock you a[nd per]secute you, plotting to kill you. I have a city, | quite small but [majestic, which is satisfactory for both of us. The Reply of the Savior: Blessed | are you because you believed [in me not having s]een me. [F]or it is w[r]it[t]en about me that those who have se | en me will not believ[e in me so that those] who have not seen might themselves believe and will live. |

22. Anderson, "Pontica," 156–58.
23. Anderson, "Pontica," 157.
24. Illert, *Doctrina Addai*, 182–83

Now, about what you wrote to me, that I come to you: it [is] nece[ssary] for me to fulfill everything for which I was sent here | and after thus fulfilling it, to be taken up to the one who sent me. But when I have been taken up, | I will send to you one of my disciples who will heal your [suff]ering and will give eternal life | and peace to those with you and to your city so that none of | your e[n]e[m]ies will gain control over it. Amen.

3.4 Philippi

A Greek inscription was found in Philippi in 1914 by Franciscan archaeologists consisting of twelve fragments, nine of which contain Abgar's letter (=inscription A) and the other three Jesus' reply (=inscription B), which includes the blessing of protection over Edessa. Charles Picard dated the inscription to the fifth century. Due to its original placement over the southeastern city gate, Picard surmised that the inscription served apotropaic purposes.[25] The wording is slightly different in some places compared to other forms of the letters. In particular, the blessing of protection includes distinct phrases about having authority (*echein tēn exousian*) and causing the city to fall (*schein*). The translation below follows the reconstruction of the text by Picard.

A
[Abga]r Ouchama, the Toparch, to Jesus who has a[ppeared
in the city of J]erusalem: greeting. [vacat][26]
[I have hear]d things about you and you[r healings,
how they are accomplished] by you [without her]bs and medicines.
[For] with a [wor]d you make the blind see, the lame [walk,
and] you clean[se leper]s, and unclean [spirits
you cast out, and those suffering with lo]ng-term ailmen[ts you heal, and
[you even raise the dead. When I hea]rd al[l these things about you, one of two
things I determined] [vacat]
either you are God [who has descended from heaven, or a Son of God who has done]
these things. Behold, [writing now I beseech you to make haste to me]
and [to heal my] suffering [for I have heard that the Jews are mock]

25. Picard, "Un texte nouveau," 65; Illert, *Doctrina Addai*, 47.
26. "Vacat" designates a long space or line left blank in the inscription.

ing you and mis[treating(?) you. I have a city,]
very sma[ll but majestic, which is satisfactory for both of us.]
B
[The reply of Jesus through Ananias the courier]:
Blessed is the one who believes in me not having seen me. For it is written
about me that those who have seen me do not believe in me
so that those who have not seen me might themselves believe and thus
[shall l]iv[e. Now about what you wrote to me, to come
to] you: it is n[ecessary for me] to fulf[ill everything for which I was sent
her]e [and after li]fe to be t[aken up
to the on]e who se[nt me. And wh]en I have been ta[ken up
. . . to my Father, I will se]nd to y[ou one of my disciples
so that he might heal your suffering and that li]fe etern[al]
and peace to your ci]ty [and to those] with you he might im[part.
And he will make your ci]ty [secure] so that [none of
your enemies can ever have authority over i]t [or cause it to fall].

3.5 Ephesus

Austrian archaeologists discovered a Greek inscription containing the Abgar/Jesus correspondence in Ephesus in 1899. It was found on the underside of a marble lintel above a courtyard entrance to a private home.[27] The inscription dates to the fifth century and contains the blessing of protection.[28] There are several unique aspects of this inscription, including using the term *despotēs* to refer to Jesus rather than the typical *kyrios* (line 7). There appears to be an error in line 8 of the inscription: the omission of the negative particle ("those who have *not* seen me"). The phrasing of the blessing of protection here is similar to the one in the Philippi inscription. The translation follows the reconstruction by Wankel, also printed in Illert's edition.

Abgar Ouchama, Toparch, to Jesus the Good Savior, who appeared in the city of Jerusalem: greeting. I have heard about you and about your healings, how without

27. Wankel, *Inschriften von Ephesos*, 285–91.
28. Illert, *Doctrina Addai*, 47.

medicines and plants they are accomplished by you. You make the blind
see, the lame walk, you cleanse lepers, and you cast out unclean spirits
and demons,
and you heal those who suffer from long-term ailments, and you raise the
dead. And hearing all of these things about you I determined in my
mind one of two things:
either that you are the Son of God and having descended from heaven you
do these things, or you are God and having descended from heaven you
do these things. For this reason I am writing
to beseech you to make haste to me and to heal the suffering I have. For I
have heard that the Jews mock you and are plotting to do you harm. But
I have a city,
very small and majestic, which is sufficient for both of us."
The reply from the Lord through Ananias the courier:
Blessed is the one who believes in me not having seen me. For it has been
written about me, those who have seen me will not believe in my and
those who have [not] seen me
will believe and they will li[v]e. But about what you wrote to me, to come
to you: i[t i]s necessary that I fulfill everything for which I was sent, and
after I fulfill
all things to be taken up to the one who sent me. And when I have been
taken up, I will send one of my disciples who will heal your
suffering and impart life to you and to all those with you, and to your city,
[so that] none of your enemies may ever hold authority over it or cause
it to fall.

3.6 Ankara Inscription

Bastiaan Van Elderen discovered this Greek inscription and published it in
1972.[29] The text is very fragmentary and difficult to reconstruct, but notably
contains a number of allusions to various Christian texts. It dates to the
fifth or sixth century. Mitchell provides a description:

> In the first section (ll. 1–10) a number of edifying examples from
> Biblical or Apocryphal literature are quoted, and they are evi-
> dently designed to serve as a guide to the behavior which we (that

29. Van Elderen, "New Inscription." See also Mitchell, "Notes and Studies No. 1,"
93–96; and Illert, *Doctrina Addai*, 47–48.

is the audience which the author addresses) should follow. Each
of these examples, except the first where the text is incomplete, is
introduced by the phrase ὁμοίως δὲ καί."[30]

The nature of this inscription is of interest in and of itself, but I restrict the focus here to the Abgar material in particular. The author holds up Abgar as an example of Christian practice and has clear knowledge of both the Abgar/Jesus correspondence as well as of the promise of divine protection. The mention of the Magi (l. 8) and of gentiles more broadly (l. 10), combined with mention of Abgar suggest that this message is directed at those who live outside the center of the empire, particularly to the east. The translation below follows the reconstruction of Mitchell. See also some of the helpful notes in Illert's edition.

] his own clothes and . . . *asen*[
] he received with pleasure the interminabl[e
forev]er. In a similar way, Jacob[31] hastened (and) offered [
] the city of the God Christ and from him received blessing and bread from
    heav[en
]*ēn* with the holy angels forever. In a similar way, Abga[r of
Ede]ssa, through a letter sent a message to the holy city of the God Christ [
]*s* walled the city of Edessa so that unshaken and unconquered i[t
]this forever. In a similar way, the Magi, hastening, offered [gifts
] city of [the God Christ.] Because they did these things, he thus promised
    them [
thou]sands to save from the gentiles. We, too, ought these same things to
    d[o
]*in* our elders from eternal judgment and we might gain salvation [
for]saking the holy city of the God Christ. For practicing these things [
bitt]er tears flow crying out, "Lord, Lord! Open for us!" [
]*sin* hear from the righteous judge: "I do not know you, who you are. Go
    away
[f]rom me."

30. Mitchell, "Notes and Studies No. 1," 94.
31. Or perhaps "James."

4 Papyri

4.1 Papyrus Gotshenburg 21

The sixth- or seventh-century Greek papyrus Gothenburg 21 likely originated in Egypt and may have been worn in an amulet.[32] The final line, as
Herbert Youtie suspects, has an incantational quality to it that is comparable to what is commonly found in the Greek Magical Papyri. The apotropaic properties and powers of a statement presumed to be written directly
by the hand of Jesus would undoubtedly have been taken for granted by
the wearer of such an amulet.[33] This fragment of the letter of Jesus demonstrates the ubiquity of the Abgar story and the popularity of the promise of
divine protection. Below I have reproduced translations based on two different reconstructions. The first comes from Youtie's 1930 essay. The second
comes from E.N. Meshtcherskaya's 1984 Russian study of *Doctr. Addai* and
the Abgar legend as a whole.[34] The two reconstructions differ in certain
areas quite significantly.

Reconstruction A

T]o Abgar, [ki]ng of Edessa, Jesus Christ the Son of God [and Son of
    Mary:[35] greet-
in]g. You are blessed. It will be well for you. And blessed is your cit[y be-
    cause] you believed. You and your people will be blessed for[ever
in] your city. And may [the light of the earth] spring up shini[ng forth] in
    it [
] I, Jesus, have written in my own hand. I comma[nd to put away al-
togeth]er blatant sin and wherever my [letters] may be cast, [whether in
. . .]*keimeno*[*is* . . .]

32. See Frisk, *Papyrus grecs*, 41; Youtie, "Gothenburg Papyrus," 302; and Illert, *Doctrina Addai*, 59. My thanks to my Greek student Gabriel Laskey for his work on this
fragment. Our conversations together were very fruitful and inspiring.

33. See Given, "Utility and Variance."

34. Meshtcherskaya, *Legenda ob Avgare*.

35. Youtie, "Gothenburg Papyrus," 300: "The name of Jesus in the form here em-
ployed—Ἰησοῦς Χριστὸς Υἱὸς Θεοῦ—occurs elsewhere in the correspondence only in
Epistula Abgari, where it is completed with καὶ υἱὸς Μαρίας. The text of Eusebius does
not have the name of Jesus within the body of the letter. The other versions of the letter
properly so called follow Eusebius with some change and addition. Hence I have though
best to fill the lacuna by writing the complete name as it is read in *Epistula Abgari*."

Reconstruction B

Jesus Christ t]o Abgar, King of Edessa: Jesus Christ the Son of the living
Go[d, to King Abgar:
greet]ing. You are blessed. It will be well for you. And blessed is your city.
[Because
in me] you believed, you and your people will be blessed forever
[Peace be] on your city. And may [the power of this letter] spring up in it,
shin[ing forth]
[(the letter) which] I, Jesus, have written in my own hand. I command [you
to remove al-
l you]r sins and wherever the[se letters] of mine may be cast,
[no power of the ad]versar[y shall approach nor gain power over the place.]

4.2 Cairo and Oxford Papyri

In a 1971 article, Rolf Peppermüller compared two papyrus fragments containing the Abgar/Jesus correspondence: P. Cair. 10736 and P. Oxf. Bodl.
MS gr. th. b 1 (P).[36] In his reconstruction of the fragments, Peppermüller
concluded that the two fragments bear witness to a variant of the correspondence that, in his assessment, predates the form of the letters in *Doctr.
Addai* and he took them as evidence of a pre-Eusebian form of the correspondence. The two fragments date to the sixth or seventh century and
contain some notable variations from other forms of the letters. Important
for Peppermüller's hypothesis is that the verso of P. Oxf. Bodl. MS gr. th.
b 1 (P) appears to lack the blessing of divine protection. If it does indeed
lack the blessing, then this would be a witness comparable in significance
only to Eusebius in the history of transmission. My translation follows Peppermüller's reconstruction of both papyri.

P. Cair. 10736

... [and they came to a meeting with their lord]
[who had sent them], King Abgar,
[and handed over the reply] of the writings[37] havin[g] be[e]n delivere[d]
by them.
[And after] they read these things, they started from the beginn-

---

36. Peppermüller, "Griechische Papyrusfragmente."
37. Grk. γραμμάτων

[ing and they spo]ke before the king all of the deeds having been performe[d]
    by Christ
[in Jerusalem] before him,
[Ananias the courier], everything he had written down
[(and) brought along. Hea]ring (all of this), King Abgar was confounded
[along with the nobles stand]ing with him. [And
Abgar said to them]

P. Oxf. Bodl. MS gr. th. b 1 (P), Recto

. . . ["for this reason, therefor]e
[I have written to beseech you to make an effort to come] to me
[and to heal the suffering I have for I ha]ve also heard that
[the Jews are mocking you and] persecuting you
[and seek to harm you. I have a city which] is very small
[(and) beautiful that is sufficient for both of us to live." When Jesus received]
[the letter in the house of the high priest of the Jews]
[he said to Ananias the courier, "Go and]
[to your master who sent you to me] say, [therefore] these things

P. Oxf. Bodl. MS gr. th. b 1 (P), Verso

["Bless]ed are you because you believed in me not [having see]n me
for [it has been writte]n about me that those who have seen me will not be-
[lieve i]n me and those who have not seen me they will
[belie]ve and they will live. But concerning what you wrote to me
[that I come to you, it is necessary] to fulfill everything for which I was
sent he[r]e and after the fulfillment
to be taken up to the one who sent me.
a[nd w]hen I have been take[n up I will send to y]ou one of
my discip[les so that he might he]al you
and impart life an[d peace to you and yours
. . . *pole* . . . *ōn*

4.3 Nessana Papyrus

The last papyrus witness comes from Nessana (modern Auja al-Hafir in the
Negev Valley on the border of Israel and Egypt). It was discovered in 1937

and later published in a collection by Lionel Casson and Ernest Hettich.[38] It is dated to the sixth or seventh century. Most notably, this is the earliest witness to the version of the Abgar/Jesus correspondence found in the *Epistles of Christ and Abgar* (*Epistula Abgari*) traditions, which are most famously connected to the legends of the Mandylion or Image of Edessa and the *Acts of Thaddaeus*.[39] This version of the letters, particularly of Jesus' reply to Abgar, contains significantly more material, including the apotropaic acclamation at the end that contains a number of *nomina sacra*. Andrew Palmer notes that the Nessana papyrus is the earliest extant witness to this cluster of *nomina sacra* and that the presence of this acclamation, along with the claim that it was composed by Jesus' own hand, could have arisen in response to the doubts about the authenticity of the correspondence raised by historians like Procopius and Evagrius Scholasticus.[40] My translation is based on the reconstruction of the Greek text by Casson and Hettich.

Gre[et]ing. I ha[ve] hea[rd] things about yo[u and your healings, how]
without med[i]ci[nes and] pla[n]ts [they are accomplished by you. For, so they]
say, you make the blind t[o] se[e, the lame to walk]
and you clea[nse] the lepers and uncl[ean spirits and dem]ons
you cast out, and tho[se] who suf[fe]r with long-term ail[ments] you heal,
and you even r[ai]se the dead. And [hearin]g al[l the]s[e thing]s about you,
I determined in my mind one of two things: either that you are God and having
come down from heaven you do these things, or you are the Son of God who
    d[o]es such things.
For
this reason, therefore, I am wr[i]ting to beseech you to hasten to me and
to heal the suffering which I have. For I have also heard that the J[ews]
mock you and are plotting to harm you. I have a ci[ty]
very s[m]all and majestic, which is su[i]tab[l]e for both of us.

The Letter of Jesus Ch[rist] the Son of God (to) Abgar, Toparch of the city of
    Edessa:
Blessed are you and your city which is called Edessa. And ble[s]sed are you
because you have believed in me even though you have not at all seen me. For
    it has been written about

38. Casson and Hettich, *Excavations at Nessana*, 143–47. The papyrus is currently housed at the Pierpont Morgan Library, cataloged as Colt Pap. 7.

39. See Palmer, "Les Actes de Thaddée."

40. Palmer, "Les Actes de Thaddée," 77 n. 37. See also Illert, *Doctrina Addai*, 60–61.

me, those who have seen me do not believe in me, so that as many as have not
    seen me
might believe and have life in me. Since, therefore, you have believed
in me, your health shall be restored to you in full. Now, concerning what you
    wrote to me
to come to you: it is necessary to fulfill the reason for which I was sent here
by my Father, and after I fulfill (it) to be taken up
to my Father who sent me. But I will send to you one of
my disciples who is the one who will heal your suffering and will impart
eternal life and peace to you and to all those with you. And he will provide
    your ci[ty]
a guarantee so that none of [your] enemies will gain control of it
until [ca. 32 letters]*mou* [ca. 11 letters]
[ca. 50 letters]
[ca. 11 letters] [there]fore I have [writt]en in full this le[tter]
[ca. 20 letters]*astēs* [w]ith a [s]eal I have se[al-]
[ed it. And they are se]t below: X, N, M, Γ

3

Appendix B

Further Developments of the Abgar/Jesus Tradition

IN THE SIXTH CENTURY and beyond, the Abgar/Jesus correspondence played an important role in the development of the traditions surrounding the story of the Image of Edessa and the Mandylion. These traditions are, in turn, related to the *Acts of Thaddaeus*. Here, I cannot parse out the complexities of these traditions and their development with any sufficiency.[1] I only offer a translation of three of these later developments of the Abgar/Jesus correspondence to demonstrate how the contents of the letters shifted for new purposes, audiences, and to serve new interests.

1. *Acts of Thaddaeus*

The *Acts of Thaddaeus* is a short Greek narrative that begins with the Abgar/Jesus correspondence and then follows the journey of Labbaeus Thaddaeus, a Hebrew from Edessa, who travels to Palestine to follow John the Baptist. After he witnesses the teachings and miracles of Jesus, however, Thaddaeus becomes one of the twelve apostles of Jesus. Meanwhile, back in Edessa, Abgar sends his courier Ananias to find out about Jesus and deliver Abgar's letter to him. *Acts Thad.* likely emerged in its current form some time in the seventh century, though Andrew Palmer has argued strongly

---

1. See Palmer, "Les Actes de Thaddée"; and Palmer, "*Logos* of the Mandylion"

for the existence of a sixth-century Syriac original that was then translated into Greek, probably in connection with the visit of Emperor Heraclius to Edessa in 629 CE.[2] The version of the Abgar/Jesus correspondence differs in substantial ways from *Doctr. Addai* and other early versions. For one, Jesus' response to Abgar is a *spoken* response, rather than a written one. The written response in this instance has been supplanted by the miraculous Mandylion, the image of Jesus' face that becomes imprinted upon a cloth. This cloth is brought back to Edessa where it purportedly remained until it was translated to Constantinople in 944 CE.[3] For my partial translation I have followed the new version of *Acts Thadd.* reconstructed by Palmer.[4]

2 In those times there was a certain toparch of Edessa named Abgar. When rumor about Christ went forth, of the marvels which he performed and of his teachings, Abgar was amazed when he heard. And he longed to see Christ, but he was not able to leave his city and rule. In the days of (Christ's) passion and the plotting of the Jews, Abgar, suffering from an incurable disease, sent a letter to Christ through Ananias the courier containing what follows:

"To Jesus, the one called Christ, from Abgar the toparch of the region of Edessa, an unworthy slave. I have heard of the multitude of wonders performed by you, that the sick and the blind, the lame and the mad and the demon-possessed are all healed. For this reason, I urge your goodness to come to us and to flee from the plotting of the abominable Jews, which in malice they set in motion against you. I have a small city, sufficient for the both of us." Abgar ordered Ananias to investigate thoroughly the nature of (Christ's) appearance—his age, his hair, and everything else.

3 When Ananias came and delivered the letter, he was staring intently at Christ, but he was unable to comprehend him. When the Knower of Hearts realized this, he asked to wash. A four-layered cloth was given to him and when he washed, he left an impression of his face. When his image was imprinted on the cloth, he handed it over to Ananias saying, "Go and give and announce to the one who sent you: peace to you and your city! For it is for this reason that I have come: to suffer on behalf of the world and to rise

2. See Palmer, "*Logos* of the Mandylion," 146–54.

3. On the translation of the relic see the *Narratio de imagine edessena* (*Story of the Image of Edessa*). Text and German translation in Illert, *Doctrina Addai*, 76–89, 260–311; English translation by Nathan J. Hardy in *MNTA* 3:65–109.

4. Palmer, "*Logos* of the Mandylion," 171–74.

again, and to raise up our first parents.[5] But after I have been taken up into heaven, I will send to you my disciple Thaddaeus who will enlighten you and guide both you and your city in the whole truth."

2. *Acts of Mār Māri*

Near the end of the sixth or the beginning of the seventh century, Christians in Mesopotamia adapted and assimilated the story of Addai and recalibrated it to fit a new narrative of Christian expansion and missionization in Mesopotamia.[6] This narrative, the *Acts of Mār Māri*, coopts the story of Addai to some degree, but also subverts it in important ways, most noticeably by replacing Addai's legacy, passed down through Aggai and Palūt in *Doctr. Addai*, with Māri, who is appointed by Addai to evangelize Mesopotamia. The complex relationship between *Doctr. Addai* and *Acts Māri* allows a glimpse at the process by which one mythological narrative is captured and assimilated by another mythological narrative to fit the purposes of a new audience and new objectives.

The text of the Abgar/Jesus correspondence in *Acts Māri* is quite close to *Doctr. Addai*, though there are places in the Syriac where changes in syntax appear to favor a Greek *Vorlage*, rather than a direct adaptation from *Doctr. Addai* itself. Certain phrases, such as the final line of Abgar's letter, have more in common with the Greek versions of the correspondence than with *Doctr. Addai*. *Acts Māri*, however, has clear knowledge of *Doctr. Addai* and acknowledges Addai as the apostle sent to Edessa. The obvious editing of the letters may be due to the desire on the storyteller's part to assimilate *Doctr. Addai* into the new story, which, while acknowledging the primacy of Edessa, intends to shift the center of gravity of Christian missionization further east into Mesopotamia.[7] I have relied on the critical text edited by Christelle and Florence Jullien.

2 In that time in which the plan of the Savior was happening, news of the healing power of Christ our Savior spread as far as to Abgar, the lord of the city of Urhay. This man had a serious disease which constantly tormented

5. Grk. προπάτορες, perhaps referring to Adam and Eve. See Palmer, "*Logos* of the Mandylion," 179, n. 171.

6. See Jullien and Jullien, *Les Actes de Mar Mari*, 13–55; Ramelli, "First Evangelization"; Ramelli, "Narrative Continuity"; and Harrak, *Acts of Mār Mārī*. On the recalibration of narratives, see Lincoln, *Gods and Demons*, 51–62.

7. See Jullien and Jullien, "Édesse dans les Actes de Mâr Mâri."

him—a disease of gout. He heard about our Savior, that he performed miracles and wonders, so he wrote him a letter and sent him envoys and messengers so that he might come to him and perform a healing on him. He wrote to him in his letter as follows:

"Abgar Ukkāmā, chief of the land, to Jesus the Savior, peace. I have heard[8] that you cleanse lepers, cast out unclean spirits, and drive out demons, and I think that you are God or the Son of God who has brought healing to creation. I have an obstinate illness and I beg of you to come to me and heal this disease. I have also heard that the Jews among your people hate you and are seeking to harm you. If you wish, I have a small city which is suitable for me and for you and sufficient for both of us, and in it there will be rest."

And the messengers went and entered Jerusalem on the twelfth of the month of Nisan. They found Christ at the house of one of the chief priests of the Jews and the letter was read before him. But our Lord was not in a position to send messengers to him, nor did he think that his gospel should go forth to the gentiles before his resurrection. For this reason, he did not send apostles to him. But he composed a letter of reply for him and wrote a greeting as follows:

"It has been written about me: 'Blessed are those who have not seen me but have believed in me.' But right now, I am seeking to complete the work for which I was sent. But after my resurrection and after my ascension into heaven, I will send to you one of my disciples who will heal your disease and give life to you and to all those who are with you. And your city will be blessed and no enemy shall have authority in it."

3 The letter came to King Abgar and he received it with great joy. When they narrated to him the wonders performed by (Christ) in the land of Judea, (Abgar) was amazed and wondered at the might of God. And since he was not worthy to see this, he felt a great sadness. So, what did King Abgar do? He found skilled painters and commanded them to go with his messengers and paint and bring the depiction of the face of our Lord, so that he might rejoice in his image as if he was in his presence. So the painters arrived with the king's messengers but they were unable to paint a depiction of the noble humanity of our Lord. When our Lord perceived, in his divine

8. Syr. *šmyʿa li*, which is a passive participle followed by a personal pronoun (lit. "it is heard by me"). This follows the Greek phrasing of ἤκουσταί μοι, a perfect passive followed by a dative personal pronoun. By contrast, *Doctr. Addai* has *šmʿat*, a simple peʿal perfect in the first person ("I have heard").

understanding, the love which Abgar had for him, and saw that the painters labored to find (his) image to paint him as he was, but were unable, he took a cloth and wiped his face, which gives life to the world, and it looked just as he was. And that cloth was brought and placed in the church of Edessa (where it remains) to this day as a source of acts of healing.

3. The *Epistles of Christ and Abgar*

The version of the Abgar/Jesus correspondence known as the *Epistles of Christ and Abgar* (*Epistula Abgari*) has been studied most carefully in connection with the legends of the image of Christ. Dates for the origin of this tradition range from after the transfer of the letters from Edessa to Constantinople in 1032[9] to, more recently, the sixth century[10]—dates which, alternatively, would place this tradition either near the beginning or at the end of the development of the legends of the image of Christ. The transmission of the *Ep. Chr. Abg.* tradition has also been contested, with some assuming a Syriac *Vorlage*[11] beneath the Greek text and others claiming Greek origins.[12] At the very least it is safe to conclude that the *Ep. Chr. Abg.* tradition is most obviously related grammatically and in terms of contents with the inscriptions from Ephesus and Edessa, and with the Nessana papyrus. Moreover, it shares some affinities with *Acts Thad.* and, interestingly, with *Acts Māri*.[13] Lipsius first published a critical text of *Ep. Chr. Abg.* in 1891.[14] For the present translation, however, I have relied on the text reconstructed by Ernst von Dobschütz in 1900.[15]

The letter written by Abgar the toparch and sent to Jesus Christ, through Ananias the courier, in Jerusalem:

Abgar, the toparch, to Jesus the Good Savior who has appeared in Jerusalem: greeting. I have heard about you and your healings, how you perform healings without medicines and herbs. With a word only, you allow the blind to see, the lame to walk; you purify lepers, and you cast out

---

9. Von Dobschütz, "Briefwechsal zwischen Abgar und Jesus."

10. Karaulashvili, "Date of the Epistula Abgari."

11. Von Dobschütz, "Der Briefwechsal zwischen Abgar und Jesus."

12. Meshtcherskaya, *Legenda ob Avgare*.

13. Karaulashvili, "Date of the Epistula Abgari," 98–109.

14. Lipsius and Bonnet, *Acta apostolorum apocrypha*, 1:281–85.

15. Von Dobschütz, "Briefwechsal zwischen Abgar und Jesus," 438–43.

unclean spirits, and you heal those who suffer from long-term ailments. You healed a hemorrhaging woman who touched you, and you raised the dead. And when I heard these things about you, I considered in my heart that you are one of two things: either you are God who has descended from heaven and you do these things, or you are the Son of God who does these things. For this reason, I beg you through letters and beseech you to come to me—though I am unworthy!—so that you might heal the suffering I have. I have also observed that the Jews mock you and are plotting to harm you. Therefore, I have a city, very small (but) majestic, which is suitable for both of us.

The reply from Jesus Christ sent to Abgar through Ananias the courier: Blessed are you, Abgar, and (blessed) is your city which is called Edessa, because you have believed in me not having seen me. Now, about what you wrote to me, to come to you: it is necessary for me to fulfill first the reason for which I was sent by the one who sent me, and after I have fulfilled it to be taken up to the Father who sent me. But after I have been taken up, I will send to you one of my disciples named Thaddaeus, who will heal your suffering and impart eternal life to you and to all those with you. And he will provide your city a guarantee that none of your enemies will overpower it until the end of the world. For it has been written about me: 'blessed are those who have seen me and believe; triple-blessed are those who have not seen me and believe.' Health of your whole soul and body is prepared for you and your house for the salvation of those who see you. For I bent the heavens and came down for the sake of the race of humankind, and I dwelt in a virgin womb so that I might obliterate the transgression that occurred in paradise. I have humiliated myself in order to magnify you humans. Wherever this letter is brought forth, whether on the road, or in the sea, or in the court, whether they are shivering, or have a fever, or have the chills, or vomiting, or under a spell, or bloated (?), or drugged, or anything like these, they will be parted from them. Let the one who bears it be pure, set apart from every evil deed and let him read it in order for there to be healing and certain joy. For this reason, this whole letter has been written in my own hand with my seal. I have sealed the letter with seven seals which are set below:

+ Ψ Χ Ε Υ Ρ Δ

Jesus Christ, the Son of God and the son of Mary, the bringer of life, the one who is known in two natures: God and human.

The interpretation of the seals is this:

The + is clear, because I was fixed to the cross;

The Ψ because I am not a mere[16] human being, but a human being in truth;

The X because I have rested over the Cherubim;[17]

The E: I[18] am the first God, and I am after these and apart from me there is no other God;

The Υ: the lofty[19] heaven and the God of Gods;

The P: I am the deliverer[20] of the race of humankind;

The Δ: I give life and I remain entirely, unceasingly, and through everything,[21] forever.

These seals, therefore, which I have marked in the letter, are the marks of the slabs which were given to Moses.

16. Grk. ψιλός
17. Grk. χερουβίμ
18. Grk. ἐγώ
19. Grk. ὑψηλός
20. Grk. ῥύστης
21. Grk. δι᾽ ὅλου καὶ διηνεκῶς καὶ διὰ παντός

Bibliography

Texts and Translations

Alichan, Léonce, ed. *Labubneay diwanagir dpri Edesioy t'ught' Abgaru: yegheal yasorwoyn i dzern s. t'argmanch'ats'*. Venice: Impr. mekhitariste de S. Lazare, 1868.

———, trans. *Lettre d'Abgar, ou Histoire de la conversion des Édesséens: Par Laboubnia, écrivain contemporain des apôtres: Traduit sur las version arménienne du Ve siècle*. Venice: Impr. mekhitariste de S. Lazare, 1868.

Anderson, J. G. C., ed. "Pontica." *JHS* 20 (1900) 151–58.

Casadei, Monica. *Didascalia di Addai. Introduzione, traduzione e note*. Testi dei Padri della Chiesa 87. Monastero di Bose: Qiqajon, 2007.

Carrière, Auguste. *La légende d'Abgar dans l'"Histoire d'Arménie" de Moïse de Khoren*. Paris: Imprimerie nationale, 1895.

Casson, Lionel, and Ernest L. Hettich, eds. *Excavations at Nessana*, vol. 2: *Literary Papyri*. Princeton: Princeton University Press, 1950. (143–47)

Cumont, Franz, ed. "Nouvelles inscriptions du Pont." *REG* 15 (1902) 311–15.

Cureton, William, ed. and trans. *Ancient Syriac Documents Relative to the Earliest Establishment of Christianity in Edessa and the Neighbouring Countries*. London: Williams & Norgate, 1864. (5–23 [text, Syriac numbering], 6–23 [trans.])

Desreumaux, Alain, trans. *Histoire du roi Abgar et de Jésus*. Apocryphes 3. Turnhout: Brepols, 1993.

Dobschütz, Ernst von, ed. "Der Briefwechsel zwischen Abgar und Jesus." *ZWT* 43 (1900) 422–86.

Elderen, Bastiaan Van, ed. "A New Inscription Relating to Christianity at Edessa." *CTJ* 7.1 (1972) 5–14.

González Núñez, Jacinto, ed. and trans. *La Leyenda del rey Abgar y Jesús: Orígenes del cristianismo en Edesa*. Apócrifos cristianos 1. Madrid: Ciudad Nueva, 1995.

Gottheil, R. J. H., ed. and trans. "An Arabic Version of the Abgar-Legend." *Hebraica* 7.4 (1891) 268–77.

Haile, Getatchew, ed. and trans. "The Legend of Abgar in Ethiopic Tradition." *OCP* 55 (1989) 375–410.

Harrak, Amir, ed. and trans. *The Acts of Mār Mārī the Apostle*. WGRW 11. Atlanta: Society of Biblical Literature, 2005.

Howard, George, ed. and trans. *The Teaching of Addai*. SBLTT 16/4. Chico, CA: Scholars, 1981.

Illert, Martin, ed. and trans. *Doctrina Addai. De imagine Edessena / Die Abgarlegende. Das Christusbild von Edessa*. Fontes Christiani 45. Turnhout: Brepols, 2007.

Jullien, Christelle, and Florence Jullien, trans. *Les Actes de Mar Mari: L'apôtre de la Mésopotamie*. Apocryphes 11. Turnhout: Brepols, 2001.

————, eds. *Les Actes de Mār Mārī*. CSCO 602–603, Syr. 234–235. Leuven: Peeters, 2003.

Langlois, Victor, trans. *Collection des historiens anciens et modernes de l'Arménie*. Paris: Didot, 1867–1869. (1:317–25)

Leloir, Louis, trans. *Écrits apocryphes sur les apôtres*. CCSA 4–5. 2 vols. Turnhout: Brepols, 1992. (2:687–704)

Lipsius, Richard A., ed. "Epistula Abgari." In vol. 1 of *Acta apostolorum apocrypha*, edited by Richard A. Lipsius and Maximilian Bonnet, 279–83. 2 vols. in 3 parts. Leipzig: Mendelssohn, 1889–1903.

McGowan, Anne, and Paul F. Bradshaw, trans. *The Pilgrimage of Egeria: A New Translation of the Itinerarium Egeriae with Introduction and Commentary*. Collegeville, MN: Liturgical, 2018.

Meshtcherskaya, Elena H., ed. *Legenda ob Avgare. Rannesirijskij literaturnyi pamjatnik*. Moscow: Nauka, 1984.

Nau, François, ed. "Une inscription grecque d'Édesse. La lettre de N.S.J.-C. à Abgar." *Revue de l'Orient Chrétien* 21 (1918) 217–18.

Oez, Mikael, trans. *I Malfonuto dAday u Şliḥo*. London: Modern Aramaic Press, 2019.

Outtier, Bernard, ed. and trans. "Une forme enrichie de la Légende d'Abgar en arménien." In *Apocryphes arméniens: transmission-traduction-creation-iconographie; Acts du colloque international sur la littérature apocryphe en langue arménienne (Genève, 18–20 septembre 1997)*, edited by Valentina Calzolari Bouvier, Jean-Daniel Kaestli, and Bernard Outtier, 129–45. Lausanne: Zébre, 1999.

Palmer, Andrew, ed. and trans. "The *Logos* of the Mandylion: Folktale, or Sacred Narrative? A New Edition of the *Acts of Thaddaeus* with a Commentary." In *Edessa in hellenistisch-römischer Zeit: Religion, Kultur, und Politik zwischen Ost und West. Beiträge des internationalen Edessa-Symposiums an Halle in der Saale, 14.–17. Juli 2005*, edited by Lutz Greisiger, Claudia Rammelt, and Jürgen Tubach, 117–207. Beiruter Texte und Studien. Beirut: Ergon, 2009.

Peppermüller, Rolf, ed. "Griechische Papyrusfragmente der Doctrina Addai." *VC* 25 (1971) 289–301.

Phillips, George, ed. and trans. *The Doctrine of Addai, the Apostle, Now First Edited in a Complete Form in the Original Syriac, with an English Translation and Notes*. London: Trübner, 1876.

Picard, Charles, ed. "Un texte nouveau de la correspondence entre Abgar d'Osroène et Jésus-Christ   grave sur une porte de ville, à Philippes (Macédoine)." *BCH* 44 (1920) 41–69.

Schwartz, Eduard, ed. *Eusebius Werke*. 2 vols. Leipzig: Hinrichs, 1903–1909.

Tchérakian, Chérubin. *Ankanon girkʻ aṛakʻelakankʻ. Tʻangaran haykakan hin ew nor dprutʻeantsʻ 3*. Venice: Ghazar, 1904. (453–63)

Walters, J. Edward, trans. "The Doctrine of Addai." In *Eastern Christianity: A Reader*, edited by J. Edward Walters, 22–35. Grand Rapids: Eerdmans, 2021.

Wankel, Hermann, ed. *Die Inschriften von Ephesos. Teil 1a Nr. 1–47 (Texte)*. Bonn: Habelt, 1979. (285–91).

Wilkinson, John, trans. *Egeria's Travels to the Holy Land*. London: SPCK, 1971.

Youtie, Herbert C., ed. "A Gothenburg Papyrus and the Letter to Abgar." *HTR* 23 (1930) 299–302.

Studies and Other Works Cited

Andrade, Nathanael J. *The Journey of Christianity to India in Late Antiquity: Networks and the Movement of Culture*. Cambridge: Cambridge University Press, 2018.

Barker, James W. "The Narrative Chronology of Tatian's Diatessaron." *NTS* 66 (2020) 288–98.

Barnes, W. Emery. "The 'Nicene' Creed in the Syriac Psalter." *JTS (Notes and Studies)* 7 (1906) 441–49.

Bauer, Walter. *Orthodoxy and Heresy in Earliest Christianity*. Philadelphia: Fortress Press, 1971. Translation of *Rechtgläubigkeit und Ketzerei im ältesten Christentum*, by Robert A. Kraft and Gerhard Krodel. BHT 10. Tübingen: Mohr Siebeck, 1934.

Blok, H. P. "Die koptischen Abgarbriefe des Leidener Museums." *AcOr* 5 (1926–1927) 248–51.

Blum, Georg G. *Rabbula von Edessa*. CSCO 200, Subs. 34. Leuven: Secrétariat du CorpusSCO, 1969.

Bovon, Francois, and Christopher R. Matthews. *The Acts of Philip: A New Translation*. Waco, TX: Baylor University Press, 2012.

Briquel Chatonnet, Françoise, and Muriel Debié, eds. *Le monde syriaque. Sur les routes d'un christianisme ignoré*. Paris: Les Belles Lettres, 2017.

Brock, Sebastian P. *The Bible in the Syriac Tradition*. Gorgias Handbooks 2. Piscataway, NJ: Gorgias, 2006.

———. "Eusebius and Syriac Christianity." In *Eusebius, Christianity, and Judaism*, edited by Harold W. Attridge and Gohei Hata, 212–34. StPB 42. Leiden: Brill, 1992.

———. *The Luminous Eye: The Spiritual World Vision of St. Ephrem the Syrian*. Kalamazoo, MI: Cistercian Publications, 1993.

———. "Studies in the Early History of the Syrian Orthodox Baptismal Liturgy." *JTS* 23 (1972) 16–64.

———. "Transformations of the Edessa Portrait of Christ." *Journal of Assyrian Academic Studies* 18 (2004) 46–56.

Brock, Sebastian P., Aaron M. Butts, George A. Kiraz, and Lucas Van Rompay, eds. *The Gorgias Encyclopedic Dictionary of the Syriac Heritage*. Piscataway, NJ: Gorgias, 2011.

Brock, Sebastian P., and David G. K. Taylor, eds. *The Hidden Pearl: The Syrian Orthodox Church and Its Ancient Aramaic Heritage*. 3 vols. Rome: Trans World Film Italia, 2001.

Buchan, Thomas. *"Blessed Is He Who Has Brought Adam from Sheol": Christ's Descent to the Dead in the Theology of Saint Ephrem the Syrian*. Gorgias Dissertations 13. Piscataway, NJ: Gorgias, 2014.

Budge, E. A. Wallis, ed. and trans. *The Book of the Bee: The Syriac Text Edited from the Manuscripts in London, Oxford, Munich, with an English Translation*. Anecdota Oxoniensia, Semitic Series 1 part 2. Oxford: Clarendon, 1886.

———, ed. and trans. *The Contendings of the Apostles, Being the Lives and Martyrdoms and Deaths of the Twelve Apostles and Evangelists*. 2 vols. London: Frowde, 1899–1901.

————, ed. and trans. *The History of the Blessed Virgin Mary and the History of the Likeness of Christ*. 2 vols. London: Luzac, 1899.

Burke, Tony, and Slavomír Céplö, trans. "The Legend of the Thirty Pieces of Silver." In *MNTA* 1:293–308.

Burkitt, F. Crawford. "Appendix to Mr. C. Winckworth's Note." *JTS* 25 (1924) 403.

————. *Early Eastern Christianity: St. Margaret's Lectures 1904 on the Syriac-speaking Church*. New York: Dutton, 1904.

————. *Evangelion da-Mepharreshe: The Curetonian Version of the Four Gospels, with the Readings of the Sinai Palimpsest and the Early Syriac Patristic Evidence*. 2 vols. Cambridge: Cambridge University Press, 1904.

Calzolari, Valentina. "The Apostle Thaddaeus in Armenian Tradition." In *The Apocryphal Acts of the Apostles in Armenian*, 29–47. Studies on Early Christian Apocrypha 18. Leuven: Peeters, 2022.

————. "Réécriture des textes apocryphes en arménien: l'exemple de la légende de l'apostolat de Thaddéé en Arménie." *Apocrypha* 8 (1997) 97–110.

Camplani, Alberto. "Traditions of Christian Foundations in Edessa: Between History and Myth." *Studi e materiali di storia delle religioni* 75 (2009) 251–78.

Castelli, Elizabeth A. *Martyrdom and Memory: Early Christian Culture Making*. New York: Columbia University Press, 2004.

Crawford, Matthew R., and Nicholas J. Zola, eds. *The Gospel of Tatian: Exploring the Nature and Text of the Diatessaron*. London: T. & T. Clark, 2019.

Debié, Muriel. "Record Keeping and Chronicle Writing in Antioch and Edessa." *ARAM* 11–12 (1999–2000) 409–17.

————. "Syriac Historiography and Identity Formation." *Church History and Religious Culture* 89 (2009) 93–114.

Den Biesen, Kees. *Simple and Bold: Ephrem's Art of Symbolic Thought*. Piscataway, NJ: Gorgias, 2014.

Desreaumaux, Alain. "La figure du roi Abgar d'Édesse." In *Edessa in hellenistisch-römischer Zeit: Religion, Kultur und Politik zwischen Ost und West: Beiträge des Internationalen Edessa-Symposiums in Halle an der Saale. 14–17 Juli 2005*, edited by Lutz Greisiger, Claudia Rammelt, and Jürgen Tubach, 31–45. Baden: Nomos, 2009.

————. "Das Neue Testament in der *Doctrina Addai*." In *Christian Apocrypha: Receptions of the New Testament in Ancient Christian Apocrypha*, edited by Jean-Michel Roessli and Tobias Nicklas, 233–48. Göttingen: Vandenhoeck & Ruprecht, 2014.

Devos, Paul. "La date du voyage d'Égérie." *AnBoll* 85 (1967) 165–94.

————. "Égérie à Edesse. S. Thomas l'apôtre. Le roi Abgar." *AnBoll* 85 (1967) 381–400.

Dewing, H. B., trans. *Procopius: History of the Wars, Books I and II*. LCL. London: Heinemann, 1914.

Doran, Robert. *Stewards of the Poor: The Man of God, Rabbula, and Hiba in Fifth-Century Edessa*. Kalamazoo, MI: Cistercian Publications, 2006.

Drijvers, Han J.W. "Addai und Mani: Christentum und Manichäismus im dritten Jahrhundert in Syrien." In *Symposium Syriacum 1980: les contacts du monde syriaque avec les autres cultures (Goslar 7–11 September 1980)*, edited by René Lavenant, 171–85. Rome: Pontificum Institutum Studiorium Orientalium, 1983.

————, ed. and trans. *The Book of the Laws of Countries: Dialogue on Fate of Bardaiṣan of Edessa*. Assen: Van Gorcum, 1965.

————. *Cults and Beliefs at Edessa*. Leiden: Brill, 1983.

———. "Facts and Problems in Early Syriac-Speaking Christianity." *SecCent* 2 (1982) 157–75.

———. "The Image of Edessa in the Syriac Tradition." In *The Holy Face and the Paradox of Representation: Papers from a Colloquium Held at the Biblotheca Hertziana, Rome and the Villa Spelman, Florence*, edited by Herbert L. Kessler and Gerhard Wolf, 13–31. Bologna: Nuova Alfa, 1998.

———. "Jews and Christians at Edessa." *JJS* 36 (1985) 88–102.

———. *Old Syriac (Edessean) Inscriptions*. Leiden: Brill, 1982.

———. "The Persistence of Pagan Cults and Practices in Christian Syria." In *East of Byzantium: Syria and Armenia in the Formative Period*, edited by Nina Garsaïan, Thomas Mathews, and Robert Thomson, 35–43. Washington, DC: Dumbarton Oaks, 1982.

———. "The Syriac Romance of Julian: Its Function, Place of Origin and Original Language." In *VI Symposium Syriacum 1992: University of Cambridge, Faculty of Divinity, 30 August–2 September 1992*, edited by René Lavenant, 201–14. Rome: Pontificum Institutum Studiorium Orientalium, 1994.

Drijvers, Han J.W., and Jan W. Drijvers. *The Finding of the True Cross: The Judas Kyriakos Legend in Syriac*. CSCO 565, Subs. 93. Leuven: Peeters, 1997.

Drijvers, Jan W. *Helena Augusta: The Mother of Constantine the Great and the Legend of Her Finding of the True Cross*. Leiden: Brill, 1992.

Duval, Rubens. *Histoire politique, religieuse et littéraire d'Édesse jusqu'à la première croisade*. Paris: Impremerie Nationale, 1892.

Eastman, David. *The Many Deaths of Peter and Paul*. OECS. Oxford: Oxford University Press, 2019.

Esbroeck, Michel van. "Le manuscrit syriaque Nouvelle Série 4 de Leningrad (Ve siècle)." In *Mélanges Antoine Guillaumont. Contributions à l'étude des christianismes orientaux*, edited by Enzo Lucchesi, 211–19. Cahiers d'Orientalisme 20. Geneva: Cramer, 1988.

———, ed. and trans. "Neuf listes d'apôtres orientales." *Aug* 34 (1994) 109–99.

Fiano, Emanuel. "The Trinitarian Controversies in Fourth-Century Edessa." *Mus* 128 (2015) 85–125.

Frisk, Hjalmar. *Papyrus grecs de la Bibliothèque Municipale de Gothembourg. (P. Got.)*. Göteborg: Elanders, 1929.

Gardner, Iain, and Samuel N.C. Lieu. *Manichaean Texts from the Roman Empire*. Cambridge: Cambridge University Press, 2009.

Given, J. Gregory. "An *Incipits* Amulet Featuring Jesus's Letter to Abgar." *JCoptS* 19 (2017) 42–49.

———. "Utility and Variance in Late Antique Witnesses to the Abgar-Jesus Correspondence." *ARG* 17 (2016) 187–222.

Giverson, Søren. "Ad Abgarum: The Sahidic Version of the Letter to Abgar on a Wooden Tablet." *AcOr* 24 (1959) 71–82.

Graf, Georg. *Geschichte der christlichen arabischen Literatur*. 5 vols. Rome: Biblioteca Apostolica Vaticana, 1944.

Griffith, Sidney H. *Asceticism*. Oxford: Oxford University Press, 1995.

———. "The Doctrina Addai as a Paradigm of Christian Thought in Edessa in the Fifth Century." *Hugoye: Journal of Syriac Studies* 6 (2003) 269–92.

———. "The Marks of the 'True Church' according to Ephraem's *Hymns Against Heresies*." In *After Bardaisan: Studies on Continuity and Change in Syriac Christianity in Honour of Professor Han J. W. Drijvers,* edited by Gerrit J. Reinink and Alex C. Klugkist, 125–40. OLA 89. Leuven: Peeters, 1999.

Guidi, Ignazio. *Chronica Minora I.* CSCO 1, Syr. 1. Leuven: Secrétariat CSCO, 1960.

Hardy, Nathan J., trans. "The Story of the Image of Edessa." In *MNTA* 3:65–109.

Harrak, Amir. "The Ancient Name of Edessa." *JNES* 51 (1992) 209–14.

———. *The Chronicle of Zuqnīn: Parts I and II from the Creation to the Year 506/7 AD.* Gorgias Chronicles of Late Antiquity 2. Piscataway, NJ: Gorgias, 2017.

Harvey, Susan Ashbrook. "Rabbula of Edessa." In *GEDSH* 348.

Hayes, Andrew. *Metrical Discourses on Faith by the Blessed Mar Ephrem. Translated, with Introduction and Notes.* Eastern Christian Texts in Translation 4. Leuven: Peeters, 2020.

Herman, Geoffrey. *Persian Martyr Acts Under King Yazdgird I.* Persian Martyr Acts in Syriac 5. Piscataway, NJ: Gorgias, 2016.

Jackson, Blomfield, trans. "The Ecclesiastical History, Dialogues, and Letters of Theodoret." In *NPNF2* 3:33–402.

Jenkins, Philip. *The Lost History of Christianity: The Thousand-Year Golden Age of the Church in the Middle East, Africa, and Asia—and How It Died.* New York: HarperOne, 2008.

Jones, Jeremiah. *A New and Full Method of Settling the Canonical Authority of the New Testament. To Which Is Subjoined a Vindication of the Former Part of St. Matthew's Gospel.* 3 vols. 1726. Reprinted Oxford: Clarendon, 1827.

Jullien, Christelle, and Florence Jullien. *Apôtres des confins. Processus missionaires chrétiens dans l'empire iranien.* Res Orientales 15. Bures-sur-Yvette: Groupe pour l'Étude de la Civilisation du Moyen-Orient, 2002.

———. "Édesse dans les Actes de Mâr Mâri." In *Apocryphité: histoire d'un concept transversal aux religions du livre. En hommage à Pierre Geoltrain.* Edited by Simon Claude Mimouni and Constantinos Macris, 167–82. Bibliothèque de l'École des Hautes Études, Sciences Religieuses 113. Turnhout: Brepols, 2002.

Karaulashvili, Irma. "The Date of the *Epistula Abgari.*" *Apocrypha* 13 (2002) 85–111.

King, Daniel, ed. *The Syriac World.* Routledge Worlds. London: Routledge, 2019.

Kitchen, Robert. A., trans. "The History of Philip." In *MNTA* 2:293–315.

Klauck, Hans-Josef. *Ancient Letters and the New Testament: A Guide to Context and Exegesis.* Translation of *Die antike Briefliteratur und das Neue Testament: Ein Lehrund Arbeitsbuch,* by Daniel P. Bailey. Waco: Baylor University Press, 2007.

Klijn, A. F. J., ed. and trans. *The Acts of Thomas.* NovT Supplement 5. Leiden: Brill, 1962.

———. "An Ancient Syriac Baptismal Liturgy in the Syriac Acts of John." *NovT* 6 (1963) 216–28.

Kohlbacher, Michael. "Rabbula in Edessa: Das Weiterwirken eines Schismas in der armenischen Bekkentnistradition." In *Blicke gen Osten: Festschrift für Friedrich Heyer zum 95. Geburtstag,* edited by Martin Tamcke, 233–74. Münster: Lit, 2004.

Landau, Brent, trans. *Revelation of the Magi: The Lost Take of the Wise Men's Journey to Bethlehem.* New York: HarperOne, 2010.

Leloir, Louis, trans. *Ephrem de Nisibe. Commentaire de l'Évangile concordant ou Diatessaron.* SC 121. Paris: Cerf, 1966.

Lightfoot, Jane L., ed. and trans. *Lucian: On the Syrian Goddess.* Oxford: Oxford University Press, 2003.

Lincoln, Bruce. *Gods and Demons, Priests and Scholars: Critical Explorations in the History of Religions.* Chicago: University of Chicago Press, 2012.

Lollar, Jacob A., ed. and trans. *The History of John the Son of Zebedee: Introduction, Texts, and Translations*. Piscataway, NJ: Gorgias, 2020.

———, trans. "The History of Paul." In *MNTA* 3:393–407.

———. "A Sanctifying Myth: The Syriac History of John in Its Social, Literary, and Theological Context." PhD diss., Florida State University, 2018.

Mar Awa Royel. "The Pearl of Great Price: The Anaphora of the Apostles Mar Addai and Mar Mari as an Ecclesial and Cultural Identifier of the Assyrian Church of the East." *OCP* 1 (2014) 5–22.

Mazzola, Marianna, and Peter Van Nuffelen. "The *Julian Romance*: A Full Text and a New Date." *Journal of Late Antiquity* 16.2 (2023) 324–77.

McCarthy, Carmel, trans. *St. Ephrem's Commentary on Tatian's Diatessaron*. Journal of Semitic Studies Supplement 2. Oxford: Oxford University Press, 1993.

McVey, Kathleen E., trans. *Ephrem the Syrian: Hymns*. CWS. New York: Paulist, 1990.

Millar, Fergus. *The Roman Near East: 31 BC–AD 337*. Cambridge: Harvard University Press, 1995.

Mingana, Alphonse, ed. and trans. "Apocalypse of Peter." In *Woodbrooke Studies: Christian Documents in Syriac, Arabic, and Garshuni*, vol. 3, edited by Alphonse Mingana, 93–449. Cambridge: Cambridge University Press, 1931.

———, ed. and trans. "The Lament of the Virgin" and "Martyrdom of Pilate." In *Woodbrooke Studies: Christian Documents in Syriac, Arabic, and Garshuni*, vol. 2, edited by Alphonse Mingana, 178–333. Cambridge: Heffer, 1928.

Mirkovic, Alexander. *Prelude to Constantine: The Abgar Tradition in Early Christianity*. Studies in the Religion and History of Early Christianity 15. Frankfurt: Lang, 2004.

Mitchell, Stephen. "Notes and Studies No. 1: Inscriptions of Ancyra." *Anatolian Studies* 27 (1977) 63–103.

Murray, Robert. "'Circumcision of the Heart' and the Origins of the *qyāmâ*." In *After Bardaisan: Studies on Continuity and Change in Syriac Christianity in Honour of Professor Han J. W. Drijvers*, edited by Gerrit J. Reinink and Alexander C. Klugkist, 201–11. OLA 89. Leuven: Peeters, 1999.

———. *Symbols of Church and Kingdom: A Study in Early Syriac Tradition*. Cambridge: Cambridge University Press, 1975. Reprint, Piscataway, NJ: Gorgias, 2006.

Norris, Richard A., Jr. *The Christological Controversy*. Sources of Early Christian Thought. Minneapolis: Fortress, 1980.

Palmer, Andrew. "Les Actes de Thaddée." *Apocrypha* 13 (2002) 63–84.

———. "King Abgar of Edessa, Eusebius and Constantine." In *The Sacred Centre as the Focus of Political Interest: Proceedings of the Symposium Held on the Occasion of the 375th Anniversary of the University of Groningen, 5–8 March 1989*, edited by Hans Bakker, 3–29. Groningen: Forsten, 1992.

Payne, Richard E. *A State of Mixture: Christians, Zoroastrians, and Iranian Political Culture in Late Antiquity*. Transformation of the Classical Heritage 56. Oakland: University of California Press, 2015.

Payne-Smith, Jessie, ed. *A Compendious Syriac Dictionary Founded upon the Thesaurus Syriacus of R. Payne Smith*. Oxford: Clarendon, 1903.

Pedersen, Nils Arne. "The Legendary Addai and the *First Apocalypse of James*." In *Ägypten und der Christliche Orient: Peter Nagel zum 80. Geburtstag*, edited by Heike Behlmer, Ute Pietruschka, and Frank Feder, 187–211. Wiesbaden: Harrassowitz, 2018.

Phenix, Robert R. Jr., and Cornelia B. Horn, ed. and trans. *The Rabbula Corpus: Comprising the* Life of Rabbula, *His Correspondence, A Homily Delivered at Constantinople, Canons, and Hymns.* WGRW 17. Atlanta: Society of Biblical Literature, 2017.

Pigulevskaya, N.V. "Katalog Siriyskikh Rukopisey Leningrada." *Palestinskiy Sbornik* 6 (69) (1960) 3–196.

Polański, Tomasz. "Translation, Amplification, Paraphrase: Some Comments on the Syriac, Greek and Coptic Versions of the *Abgar Letter.*" *Collectanea Christiana Orientalia* 13 (2016) 159–210.

Possekel, Ute. *Evidence of Greek Philosophical Concepts in the Writings of Ephrem the Syrian.* CSCO 580, Subs. 102. Leuven: Peeters, 1999.

———. "The Transformation of Harran from a Pagan Cult Center to a Christian Pilgrimage Site." *ParOr* 36 (2011) 345–56.

Ramelli, Ilaria L. E. "The First Evangelization of the Mesopotamian Regions in the Syriac Tradition: The Acta Maris as a Continuation of the Doctrina Addai." *Antiguo Oriente* 3 (2005) 11–54.

———. "The Narrative Continuity Between the Teaching of Addai and the Acts of Mari: Two Historical Novels?" In *Narratives of Egypt and the Ancient Near East: Literary and Linguistic Approaches*, edited by Fredrik Norland Hagen, et al., 411–50. OLA 189. Leuven: Peeters, 2011.

———. "Possible Historical Traces in the *Doctrina Addai.*" *Hugoye: Journal of Syriac Studies* 9.1 (2006) 51–127.

Rigolio, Alberto. "Syriac." In *How Literatures Begin: A Global History*, edited by Joel B. Lande and Denis Feeney, 167–90. Princeton: Princeton University Press, 2021.

Roggema, Barbara. "Biblical Exegesis and Interreligious Polemics in the Arabic Apocalypse of Peter—The Book of the Rolls." In *The Bible in Arab Christianity*, edited by David Thomas, 131–50. History of Muslim-Christian Relations 6. Leiden: Brill, 2007.

Ross, Steven Kirk. *Roman Edessa: Politics and Culture on the Eastern Fringes of the Roman Empire, 114–242 CE.* London: Routledge, 2001.

Rouwhorst, Gerard A.M. "The Descent of Christ into the Underworld in Early Christian Liturgy." In *The Apostles' Creed: "He Descended into Hell,"* edited by Marcel Sarot and Archibald L. H. M. van Wieringen, 54–78. Leiden: Brill, 2018.

Ruani, Flavia. "Peut-on parler de testimonia dans l'Histoire de Philippe syriaque?" In *La littérature apocryphe chrétienne et les Écritures juives*, edited by Rémi Gounelle and Benoît Mounier, 34–56. Publications de l'Institut romand des sciences bibliques 7. Lausanne: Zèbre, 2015.

Ruani, Flavia, and Émilie Villey. "Recherches sur la transmission manuscrite syriaque de l'Histoire de Philippe." In *Manuscripta Syriaca: Des sources de première main.* Edited by Françoise Briquel-Chatonnet and Muriel Debié, 385–420. Cahiers d'études syriaques 4. Paris: Geuthner, 2015.

Saint-Laurent, Jeanne-Nicole Mellon. *Missionary Stories and the Formation of the Syriac Churches.* Transformation of the Classical Heritage 55. Berkeley: University of California Press, 2015.

Schwartz, Daniel L. "Discourses of Religious Violence and Christian Charity: The Christianization of Syria in Jacob of Sarug's *On the Fall of the Idols.*" In *Motions of Late Antiquity: Essays on Religion, Politics, and Society in Honour of Peter Brown*, edited by Jamie Kreiner and Helmut Reimitz, 129–49. Turnhout: Brepols, 2016.

Segal, Judah B. *Edessa, the 'Blessed City.'* Oxford: Clarendon Press, 1970. Reprinted Piscataway, NJ: Gorgias, 2005.

Shepardson, Christine. *Anti-Judaism and Christian Orthodoxy: Ephrem's Hymns in Fourth-Century Syria.* Washington, DC: Catholic University of America Press, 2008.

Skelton, David A., and Jacob A. Lollar. "Wisdom of Solomon 15.3: Syriac." In *The Textual History of the Bible*, vol. 2: *Deutero-Canonical Scriptures*, edited by Frank Feder, Matthias Henze, and Mika Pajunen, 494–97. Leiden: Brill, 2020.

Smith, Kyle. *Constantine and the Captive Christians of Persia.* Berkeley: University of California Press, 2016.

Sokoloff, Michael, trans. *The Julian Romance.* Texts from Christian Late Antiquity 49. Piscataway, NJ: Gorgias, 2017.

Steiner, Deborah Tarn. *Images in Mind: Statues in Archaic and Classical Greek Literature and Thought.* Princeton: Princeton University Press, 2002.

Takahashi, Hidemi. "Ḥārrān." In *GEDSH*, 191–92.

———. "Nisibis." In *GEDSH* 310–11.

Tannous, Jack. *The Making of the Medieval Middle East: Religion, Society, and Simple Believers.* Princeton: Princeton University Press, 2018.

Taylor, David G. K. "The Coming of Christianity to Mesopotamia." In *The Syriac World*, edited by Daniel King, 68–87. Routledge Worlds. London: Routledge, 2019.

Teixidor, Javier. "Le thème de la descente aux Enfers chez Saint-Éphrem." *L'Orient syrien* 6 (1961) 25–41.

Torrey, C. C. "A Syriac Parchment from Edessa of the Year 243 A.D." *ZS* 10 (1935) 32–45.

Vanden Eykel, Eric. *The Magi: Who They Were, How They've Been Remembered, and Why They Still Fascinate.* Minneapolis: Fortress, 2022.

Vööbus, Arthur. *Studies in the History of the Gospel Text in Syriac.* CSCO 128, Subs. 3. Leuven: Durbecq, 1951.

Walters, J. Edward, trans. "The Preaching of Simon Cephas in the City of Rome." In *MNTA* 3:408–23.

Wardle, Timothy Scott. "Abgarids of Edessa." In *GEDSH* 5–7.

Witakowski, Witold, trans. "The Teaching of the Apostles." In *MNTA* 2:607–22.

Wright, William. *Catalogue of Syriac Manuscripts in the British Museum Acquired since the Year 1838.* 3 vols. London: British Library, 1870–1872.

———, ed. and trans. "The Departure of My Lady Mary from this World." *Journal of Sacred Literature and Biblical Record* 6 (1865) 417–48; 7 (1865) 108–60.

———. "Syriac Manuscripts at St. Petersburg, etc." *Journal of Sacred Literature and Biblical Record* NS 10.20 (1867) 461–62.

Index of Ancient Sources

**Hebrew Bible/
Old Testament**

Genesis

11:6–9   59

Exodus

34:35   40

Deuteronomy

27:15   63

2 Samuel

8:1   55

Nehemiah

8:1–8   61

Psalms

23:3   93
56/55:9   61
115:5   66
135:15–16   66
136:6   67
136:7   67

Isaiah

48:16   58
65:6   61

Daniel

4:13   56
7:10   61

Hosea

14:9   90

**Pseudepigrapha and
Intertestamental Literature**

Ascension of Isaiah
9:22–23   61

1 Enoch   56
81:1–2   61

Jubilees
5   56

Wisdom
2:21   66
13   64
13:1   66
13:16   64
14:8   63
15   62
15:15   66

Classical and Greco-Roman

Literature

Cassius Dio
Histories
    78.12.1   99

Historia Augusta
25.7   46

Josephus
Jewish Antiquities
    18.4.3   83, 85
    18.6.6   84
    20.197   83
    20.198   48
Jewish War
    4.8.1   33
    6   67

Julian (Emperor)
Orations
    4   63

Porphyry of Tyre
Vita Plotini
    1   38

Suetonius
Claudius
    5   45
    5.25   52

Tacitus
Annals
    6.32   84
    12.12, 14   43

New Testament

Matthew
2   2
4:16   69
5:12   89
5:45   62
7:14   44
7:15   44
9:20–26   59
10:3   3
10:9–10   43
10:9   97
10:38   43
11:5   36
16:16   51
16:24   43
18:10   88
19:28   87
23:3   87
23:38   67
25   56
25:14–30   87
25:14–25   60
25:31–46   44
27   56
27:25   89
27:39   49
27:51   43, 64, 67
27:52–53   67
27:52   56
28   70
28:19   43, 58, 76

Mark
1:3   88
4:1–9   60
6:11   61, 71
6:18   3
9:38   65
15:9   49
15:33–51   83
15:33   56, 59, 67
15:38   67
16:15   43
16:20   65

Luke
3:2   48
6:23   89
7   22
7:22   36
9:23   43

9:49	65
9:62	91
10	5, 39
10:1–20	2
10:1–12	39
10:17–20	39
10:4	43
13:35	67
14:27	43
19:12–27	87
19:12–23	60
22:30	87
23:33	48
24:4–7	56

John

1:13	77
1:18	97
6:38	41
11:36	95
12:40–46	66
13:17	87
14:2–3	90
17:1–5	57
17:5	41
20:29	37, 41, 68, 104

Acts

1:8–9	44
1:8	43
2	1, 2
2:1–4	44
2:6–12	59
2:43	65
4:6	48
5:18	47
5:33–39	35
7:51–52	61
7:52	89
8:3	47
12:4	47
15:4	53
17:22–34	69
18:2	52
22:3	35

Romans

1	62
1:20	62
11:30–31	62

1 Corinthians

3:23	93
7:21	93

2 Corinthians

8:9	92
12:12	65

Ephesians

2:13	65
2:17	59

Philippians

2:6–8	42
2:7	57

Hebrews

1:1	69, 90
2:14	57

James

2:1	91

1 Peter   2

2:11	90

1 John

1:3	44
2:25	93

Apocrypha

Acts of Mār Māri	25, 38, 77, 96
2–3	124–26
Acts of Paul	25
Acts of Peter	
34	83

Acts of Peter by Clement   28

Acts of Philip   2

Acts of Thaddaeus   26, 29, 111, 122–24, 126

Acts of Thomas   2, 39

Book of the Rolls   28

Gospel of Peter
35–44   56

History of John   20, 21, 45, 63, 64, 70, 78, 90
13   39
14   40
22   61
32   91

History of Paul   1, 91

History of Philip   2

History of Simon Cephas,
   Chief of the Apostles   78
29:3   46
30   83
33   100

History of the Virgin   26

Lament of the Virgin   35

Legend of the Thirty Silver Pieces   26

Martyrdom of Pilate   35

Preaching of Simon Cephas
   in the City of Rome   64, 91
10:7   100

Pseudo-Clementine Recognitions   46

1 Revelation of James   15

Revelation of the Magi   2

Six Books Dormition of Mary   26
2   47

Story of the Image of Edessa   123

Syriac Literature

Bardaisan
   Books of the Laws
     of the Countries   12, 32, 54, 72

Chronicle of Edessa   74, 99
1–2   73
3   86, 32
4   54

Chronicle of Zuqnīn   xiii
95   32
97–98   73, 99
123   41
125   41

Ephrem the Syrian
   Carmina Nisibena
     1.11   10
     33   89
     36   43
   Commentary
   on the Diatessaron   19, 57
     21.4   59
   Contra Haereses
     8.10–14   63
     9.8   63
     22.5–6   7
     41.4   63
   Contra Julianum
     1.8–15   10
   de Azymis
     3   43
   de Crucifixion
     8   43
   de Ecclesia

36	66
37	66

Discourses to Hypatius
5	93

Metrical Discourses on Faith
2	90

*History of the Man
of God from Rome* (Syriac) — 21, 22

Jacob of Serug (Batnae)
Homily on the Fall of the Idols — 62

Julian Romance	38
123–24	115

*Life and Miracles of Cosmas
and Damien* (Syriac) — 21

Life of Abraham of Qidun — 21, 22

Life of Basil of Caesarea (Syriac) — 21

Life of Ephrem	45
42	94

Life of Gregory Thaumaturgus
(Syriac) — 21

Life of Julian Sabas — 21

Life of Rabbula	18, 45
40	17

Martyrdom of Aitalāhā — 22, 53, 55

Martyrdom of Barsamya — 22, 32, 53–55, 78

Martyrdom of Habib — 93

Martyrdom of James (Jacob) Intercisus
(Syriac) — 21

Martyrdom of Narsai — 36, 56

Martyrdom of Sharbel — 21, 22, 55, 76

Martyrdom of Sophia (Syriac) — 21

Pseudo-Irenaeus of Lyon
List of Apostles and Disciples — 26

Rabbula of Edessa
*Commandments and Admonitions
for the Priests and Children of the
Covenant* — 98
11	80
12	80
16	80
17	79
24	80
34	80
43	92
44	92
53	76

Admonitions for the Monks
10	92

Solomon of Bostra
Book of the Bee
44	26
49	26

Teaching of the Apostles	31, 47, 91
3:10	78
6:9–10	77, 96
6:9	26, 55, 85

Theodore Abū Qurrah — 38

Other Late Antique Christian Literature

Actus Silvestri — 65

Augustine of Hippo
   Contra Faustum Manichaeum
   28.4 — 3

   De consensus evangelistarum
   1.7.11 — 3

   De haeresibus
   46.18 — 56

   Epistulae
   230 — 3

Codex Theodosianus
16.10.3 — 76

Cyril of Alexandria — 15, 16, 23, 80

Epistulae ad Nestorianum
2 — 41, 43, 57, 65
4 — 58, 67

Egeria
   Itinerarium — 8–10, 11, 12, 14–15, 25, 38, 51, 71, 102, 107–11
   8–9 — 9
   16 — 6
   17.2 — 35
   19 — 6
   19.2 — 78
   19.8 — 37
   19.9 — 37
   19.17 — 37
   19.19 — 35, 37

Eusebius of Caesarea
   Ecclesiastical History
   1.13 — 3, 5, 102–6
   1.13.5 — 35
   1.13.9 — 33
   1.13.11 — 39
   2.23.21 — 83
   4.3.3 — 84
   7.17–18 — 59
   9.1.2–6 — 33

   Life of Constantine — 65

   Theophania — 67

Evagrius Scholasticus
   Ecclesiastical History — 38, 120
   4.27 — 3, 25

Invention of the Cross — 21, 45, 47–48, 51–52

John of Damascus
   De Fide Orthodoxa — 26, 38

Life of Jacob of Galash — 38

Moses of Khoren — 82
   History of the Armenians
   2.26–36 — 27

Procopius
   History of the Wars
   2.12.25–26 — 3, 8

Seven Sleepers of Ephesus — 21

Theodoret
   Ecclesiastical History
   2.30 — 10, 37

Index of Names and Places

'Abdu bar 'Abdu (noble in Edessa),
40, 42, 44, 53, 54, 74, 105
Abgar (VIII the Great), 7, 32, 41, 72,
73, 74, 99, 100
Abgar Severus, 99
Abgar Ukkāmā (the Black), 4, 7, 32,
36, 41, 72, 73, 82, 99, 104,
112–14, 125
Abraham of Qidun (saint), 21, 22
'Abšelāmā, 78, 86, 93, 100
Aggai (apostle), 5, 7, 12, 26, 43, 75,
77, 86, 93, 96, 97, 99–100, 124
Antioch (Syria), 5, 7, 80, 100
archives (Edessan), 3, 5–6, 22, 31, 35,
55, 82, 101, 103
Aristides (messenger), 84
Armenia, 27, 43, 81,
'Aryū, 95
Artiqa, 84
Atargatis (Artemis, Syrian Goddess),
11, 63
Augustina (mother of Abgar), 43,
53, 73
Aulbinus (governor), 83
'Awidā (Šawida) son of 'Ebednaḥad
(noble of Edessa), 54–55, 75–
76, 78, 86

Bar Kalbā (noble of Edessa), 53, 54,
55, 75, 78, 86
Bardaisan of Edessa (Philosopher),
17, 32, 54, 69, 72
Barsmayā (priest), 78
Bāt Nikal (Ishtar), 62

Bel, 11, 62, 64, 76, 89, 98
Beth Gubrin (Eleutheropolis), 33
Beth Tbārā, 54

Caiaphas (chief priest), 48, 85
Caracalla (emperor), 99
Carrhae (*see* Ḥārrān)
Chalcedon, Council of, 16, 58, 75
Claudius (emperor), 4, 32, 45, 46, 47,
52, 81, 84, 85
Constantine the Great (emperor), 13,
43, 53, 81
Constantinople, 26, 38, 41, 67, 123,
126
Cyril of Alexandria (bishop), 15–16,
23, 41, 43, 57, 58, 65, 67, 80

Decius (emperor), 22
Diocletian (emperor), 13, 81

Eulogius of Edessa (bishop), 25, 35,
110
Euphrates, 103

Gaius (emperor), 32, 45, 81, 85
Gamaliel (chief of Jews), 35
Gedalia son of Caiaphas, 48

Ḥanan (Ananias), 9, 4, 13, 33–39, 48,
101, 104, 108–9, 114–15, 119,
122–23, 126–27
Ḥaphsai, 53, 55, 78
Ḥārrān, 55, 62, 63, 81, 89

Helena Augusta, 21, 43, 45, 46, 48,
    51, 52, 53
Herod (king), 47
Hiba (Ibas) of Edessa (priest/bishop),
    15, 80

Jacob of Nisibis (bishop), 9–10
Judah son of ʿEbed Šalom, 48
Julian (emperor), 9, 63

Lebubnā bar Senaq, bar ʿAbšadar,
    5–6, 13–14, 55, 101
Lucius Varus (emperor), 41
Lucius Vitellius (governor), 83, 85

Maʿnu, 4, 31–32, 73, 99
Mabbug (Hieropolis), 2, 63, 84
Magnus (son of Abgar), 107, 109
Māryāhb (son of Bar Šemeš), 4,
    32–33, 86

Narsai of Nisibis, 80
Narseh/Narses (king), 5, 12, 24,
    81–82
Nebo, 11, 62, 64, 76, 89, 97
Nestorius of Constantinople (bishop),
    41, 43, 57, 58, 65, 67, 80
Nicea, Council of, 9, 66
Nisibis, 9–11, 37, 55, 77, 80, 85

Onias son of Ḥanan/Ananias, 48

Palūt (bishop), 5, 7–8, 12, 14, 77, 78,
    86, 93, 100, 124
Paneas (Banias), 26, 59
Peroz (priest), 76, 86
Protonike, 4, 12, 21–22, 24–25,
    45–52, 92, 94

Rabbula of Edessa (bishop), 12,
    15–18, 22–23, 41, 45, 66, 79,
    80, 88, 91, 92, 98
Rome, 1, 2, 7, 22, 35, 41, 46, 52, 81,
    84, 91, 99, 100

Sabinus (procurator), 33
Šalmath daughter of Meherdath (wife
    of Abgar), 43, 53, 73
Šmešgrām (noble of Edessa), 4,
    32–33, 54, 55, 74
Samaritans, 68
Sassanians, 2, 37, 81
School of the Persians, 80
Seleucia-Ctestiphon, 93
Senaq bar ʿAwidā, 86, 101
Septimius Severus (emperor), 33, 41
Serapion (bishop), 5, 7, 100
Shapur I (king), 76, 81, 93
Shapur II (king), 9–10, 37
Sharbel (saint), 22, 55, 76
Sin (deity), 11, 55, 62, 63,
Šobā (*see* Nisibis)
Spain, 1, 6, 25, 46, 107
Sun (deity), 63, 89

Tarʿatha (*see* Atargatis)
Theodore of Mopsuestia, 80
Tiberius (emperor), 32, 41, 45–47,
    82–85
Tiqnutha, 84
Tobia (Tobias), 4, 34, 40, 104–5
Trajan (emperor), 22

Xanthippe (wife of Gaius), 83

Zephyrinus (bishop), 7, 100